Managing the
Global Workforce

The *Global Dimensions of Business* series provides authoritative summaries of the latest developments in international business and management.

Books in the series provide:

- focused, topic-based summaries of the key global developments in the different sub-disciplines of business
- an international perspective on the core topics in the curriculum for executive, MBA, and advanced graduate students in business
- strategic and practitioner implications in each topic area
- commentary on emergent and changing trends as well as established knowledge

Selected titles in the series:

Managing the Global Workforce

Paula Caligiuri
David Lepak
Jaime Bonache

WILEY
John Wiley & Sons, Ltd.

This edition first published 2010
© 2010 John Wiley & Sons, Ltd

Registered office
John Wiley & Sons Ltd, The Atrium, Southern Gate, Chichester, West Sussex, PO19 8SQ, United Kingdom

For details of our global editorial offices, for customer services and for information about how to apply for permission to reuse the copyright material in this book please see our website at www.wiley.com.

The right of the author to be identified as the author of this work has been asserted in accordance with the Copyright, Designs and Patents Act 1988.

Reprinted June 2010

Library of Congress Cataloging-in-Publication Data

A catalogue record for this book is available from the Library of Congress

ISBN 978-1-405-10732-7

A catalogue record for this book is available from the British Library.

Set in 10/12.5 Rotis Serif by Aptara Inc., New Delhi, India.
Printed in Great Britain by TJ International Ltd, Padstow, Cornwall

To George, Ellen, and Celia – for joining us on our global journeys

CONTENTS

ABOUT THE AUTHORS

Paula Caligiuri is Professor of the Human Resource Management Department in the School of Management and Labor Relations at Rutgers University, where she is the Director of the Center for Human Resource Strategy (CHRS). Paula is a leading expert in strategic human resource management with a focus on international management, global leadership development, and international assignee management. Paula has been recognized as one of the most prolific authors in the field of international business for her work in global careers and global leadership development and has lectured in numerous universities in the United States, Asia, and Europe.

With a focus on global careers, Paula has authored a book for general readers, *Get a Life, Not a Job* (FT Press, 2010). She is co-author with Steven Poelmans of *Harmonizing Work, Family, and Personal Life* (Cambridge University Press, 2008). She is also a popular blogger on these topics (www.PaulaCaligiuri.com). Paula's other academic publications include several articles in the *International Journal of Human Resource Management, Journal of World Business, Journal of Applied Psychology, Personnel Psychology,* and *International Journal of Intercultural Relations.* Consonant with her interest in action-oriented research, she has also published on the topic of psychometric statistics in the *Handbook of Statistics* and *Statistics and Probability.*

Paula covers management-related topics for CNN. She has also recently completed a pilot for a television show, "CareerWATCH." She is a frequent speaker for numerous academic and practitioner-oriented conferences in the United States, Asia, Australia, and

Europe. As a consultant, Paula is the President of Caligiuri and Associates, Inc., a consulting firm specializing in selection, performance assessment, and development of global leaders. Paula is the creator of The Self-Assessment for Global Endeavors (The SAGE), The SAGE for Spouses, and The SAGE for Global Business Leaders. Her clients include several US-based and European-based global organizations.

Paula holds a PhD from Penn State University in industrial and organizational psychology.

David Lepak is Professor of Human Resource Management and Chairperson of the Human Resource Management department in the School of Management and Labor Relations at Rutgers University. He received his PhD in management from the Pennsylvania State University. David is a leading scholar in the strategic management of human resources and teaches and conducts research on a variety of human resource topics with dual interests in strategic human resource management and international human resource management. He is a frequent presenter to many domestic and international audiences.

David's research interests are primarily focused on understanding how to leverage the talents of employees through human resource management systems. His specific expertise is in employment subsystems and the HR architecture, contingent labor, intellectual capital, and linking HR systems to important company outcomes. David has co-authored a comprehensive textbook with Mary Gowan, entitled *Human Resource Management* (Prentice Hall, 2008). His research has appeared in a variety of outlets such as: *Research in Personnel and Human Resource Management, Academy of Management Review, Academy of Management, Journal, Journal of Applied Psychology, Journal of Management, Human Resource, Management, Human Resource Management Review*, among others.

David is associate editor of *Academy of Management Review* and has served on the editorial boards of *Academy of Management Journal, Journal of Management, Human Resource Management, British Journal of Management*, and *Journal of Management Studies*.

Jaime Bonache is Professor of Human Resource Management at Esade Business School (Spain). He is also Visiting Professor at Cranfield School of Management (England). In 2007 he attained his habilitation as Professor of Organization Studies at Carlos III University of Madrid, the highest academic qualification in Spain. Jaime holds an MA in Philosophy from Carleton University (Ottawa, Canada), an

MBA from IADE, and a PhD in Economics and Business Administration from the Universidad Autónoma de Madrid (Spain).

Jaime's research interests are in the areas of global assignments, the international transfer of knowledge and people management systems, and strategic international human resource management. His doctoral dissertation centred on the strategic determinants of compensation practices within multinational enterprises. He has written/edited four books, two of them (*Direccion Estrategica de Personas* and *Direccion de Personas*, with Angel Cabrera), have been best-sellers in a number of Spanish-speaking countries. He has been guest editor of four special issues on trends in international human resources and published a large number of articles in leading academic journals including *Organization Studies, Human Resource Management Journal*, the *International Journal of HRM, Journal of Business Research*, and *HRM Review*. Jaime is a frequent speaker at academic and professional conferences and is widely recognized as one of Europe's leading authorities on international human resource management.

Jaime has participated in the post-graduate programmes and academic activities of numerous European and Latin-American academic institutions, and participated in Scientific Committees of the Academy of Management and other major international research institutions.

CHAPTER 1

Introduction to International Dimensions of Human Resource Management

1.1 The Global Economy and Multinational Companies

In today's highly competitive global business environment, organizations need to aggressively compete for new markets, products, services, and the like in order to develop and sustain competitive advantage in the global arena. For many years, multinational companies[1] (those operating in more than one country) have effectively managed their financial and material resources globally, leveraging such things as economies of scale, low cost production, and currency fluctuations. This book accepts the fact that the competitive economy in which most companies operate is, indeed, the *global economy*. Along with financial and material resources, firms must also compete for human resources. Human resources, like all other business resources, are now being managed on a global scale – and those firms most effectively competing for talent and unlocking their employees' potential are clearly winning a competitive advantage. This book focuses on global firms' human resources and how to most effectively manage the global workforce.

Multinational Companies' Growth and Structure. Let's begin with how firms grow their geographic reach around the world.

Every organization, with few exceptions, has a country of origin. This is generally the country of the founder's nationality and often the country where the firm's headquarters are located and to which foreign or host national subsidiaries report. This is generally the country defining the firm's domestic market and from which it will build its international market. Many, but not all, companies grow by competing first within a largely domestic market and then competing on a global scale. Organic global growth occurs as firms naturally (and relatively slowly) expand their market reach around the world by gradually expanding their markets, opening subsidiaries in other countries, spreading production and distribution locations around the world, and so forth.

Multinational firms may also grow inorganically (and relatively quickly) through mergers, acquisitions, international joint ventures, and alliances. These methods for growing globally pose a different set of challenges for HR professionals because, in addition to managing the scale and geography, there are also new HR systems to be merged, employees to be integrated, cultures to be assessed, work to be divided, and the like. In acquisitions, the acquiring firm purchases a target firm whereas mergers are the blending of two firms into one. The line between a merger and an acquisition becomes blurred as the merger departs from a 50-50 blend of two comparably sized firms. Mergers and acquisitions will occur for several possible reasons, including an attempt to consolidate and control more of an industry, to gain access to products, to gain entry into a geographical region where they are not represented, underrepresented or previously unsuccessful, to have access to the target firm's research and development, patents, licenses, and the like. Whatever the reason, there are synergies a global firm expects to achieve by acquiring or merging with another firm.

In international joint ventures and alliances there are two (or more) firms from different countries involved in a jointly owned and/or jointly operated business venture. The benefit of these international alliances and joint ventures is an expeditious expansion of global resources, at minimum, across two countries. These ventures and alliances may range from two firms creating a third, newly formed more permanent business (the typical international joint venture) to more temporary or cooperative arrangements, such as licensing and royalty or project-based agreements. In the latter, these ventures tend to include partners with complementary roles.

Whether through organic or inorganic growth, as firms expand globally, their organizational structures tend to become increasingly more complex. The most basic organizational structure of a firm operating globally has a corporate headquarters located in the company's country of origin and at least one (but often several) foreign subsidiaries. These foreign subsidiaries may perform a variety of functions, such as production, sales, administrative hubs, research and development sites, call centers, distribution centers, and so forth. Firms organize the relationships among their foreign subsidiaries – and with the headquarters – in three predominant ways: by geography, by business units, or through a matrix structure. Firms organized by geography may be organized by countries or, more typically geographic regions (e.g. the Americas, Asia, Middle East, Europe) reporting into headquarters.

There are two factors to consider which will influence a firm's organizational structure across its foreign subsidiaries. They are (1) geographic dispersion and (2) multiculturalism.[2] *Geographic dispersion* is the extent to which a firm is operating across borders and must coordinate operations across borders in order to be effective. *Multiculturalism* is the extent to which the workers, customers, suppliers, etc., are from diverse cultural backgrounds and must coordinate the activities of people from diverse cultures in order to be effective.

Operating with both geographic dispersion and multiculturalism concurrently, organizations must achieve a dynamic balance between the need to be centralized, or tightly controlled by headquarters, and the need to be decentralized, or operating differently across diverse locations.[3] Extreme centralization can provide an organization with a variety of competitive benefits such as economies of scale (and associated cost controls), improved value chain linkages, product/service standardization, and global branding. Extreme decentralization, however, can also be useful, enabling a firm to modify products or services to fully meet local customer needs, respond to local competition, remain compliant with various governments' regulations in different countries of operation, readily attract local employees, and penetrate local business networks. These two countervailing forces, centralization and decentralization,[4] will affect a firm's organizational structure by reinforcing or relinquishing central (controlled by headquarters) or local (controlled by subsidiaries) control. The level of autonomy and control each country has relative to the headquarters is a strategic issue depending on the amount of global integration and local responsiveness sought by each firm respectively.

As firms become more diversified with multiple lines of business, the strategy of the firm as a whole may be better served with each line of business operating as a relatively separate (more flexible and more responsive) entity. This is the structure of firms organized by business unit. In firms with a matrix structure, there is an acknowledgement that geographies may need some degree of local responsiveness and that the repetition of administrative activities across the business units does not leverage economies of scale for the firm as a whole. In other words, neither organizing by geography nor by business unit is, on its own, effective. The solution is for firms to structure themselves into a matrix having geographical regions embedded within business units, or vice versa. The matrix organizational structure is popular among large and mature firms operating globally. The structure, as you can imagine, is complex.

1.2   Managing Human Talent for Global Competitive Advantage

Even in the most complex organizational structure, the matrix structure, organizations' competitiveness on a global scale is largely contingent on the ability of firms to strategically adapt, reconfigure, and acquire the resources needed for the ever-changing global marketplace. Given that it is the *people* within organizations who sell and market, develop products, make decisions, and implement programs, human resources are vital to the success of an organization. The allocation of human talent worldwide and the application of human resource practices congruent with the organizations' strategic goals to help manifest the firms' strategic capabilities are a means to facilitate the successful implementation of firms' global business strategies.

Human resources, like all other resources in firms with foreign subsidiaries, should be managed on a global scale. When to move jobs? Where to move people? Whether to leverage local talent or search for talent globally? How to create synergy within units across countries? These are a few of the many human resource challenges facing firms today. We believe, as we hope to illustrate in this book, that in our ever-increasing knowledge economy, winning in the global arena will largely depend on how well firms can leverage, attract, develop, engage, and motivate the capabilities of their human talent globally.

1.3 This Book

This book was written to offer a framework for understanding the complexities of managing the global workforce. The framework introduced in this book and illustrated in Figure 1.1 is helpful for understanding the challenges and issues you must address and the decisions you must make when managing human talent on a worldwide basis. The chapters are organized around progressive themes within each of the book's two major sections. The first half of *International Dimensions of Human Resource Management* covers the three foundational areas for managing a global workforce: business strategy, comparative HR systems, and cross-cultural issues.

Focusing on global business strategy, Chapter 2 describes the strategic levers and the ways in which human resource practices

Figure 1.1 The Balance of Firm-Level Strategic Demands and the Country-Level Contextual Factors

may vary depending on the strategic goals of the transnational firm. Chapter 2 also discusses the various strategic capabilities for which global firms strive, such as global integration, local responsiveness, and worldwide innovation and learning – exploring the various ways human resource practices can facilitate these strategic capabilities. This chapter will ask and answer questions, such as: How can we gain a competitive advantage in managing a global workforce? What tasks and strategic HR decisions will we have to adopt in this area? Will we need to use the same (or a similar) system of managing workers throughout the company's international structure? What barriers or difficulties will stand in the way of its implementation? What can we do to facilitate cooperation and exchange of experiences among employees working in different subsidiaries?

Chapter 3 focuses on comparative HR systems, the various fixed aspects of countries' human resource systems, such as labor unions, educational systems, legal systems, and so forth. These dimensions are particularly relevant when transnational firms operate in multiple foreign countries (as most do), adding to the complexity of managing a global workforce. This chapter will ask and answer questions, such as: What are the cross-border differences in employment and labor laws, workforce competence (e.g. literacy rates and educational systems), labor economics, and unionization?

Chapter 4 focuses on cross-cultural differences, describing the cultural dimensions that influence the acceptance of global human resource practices, such as cross-cultural differences in management styles, time, communication, and the like. This chapter encourages readers to not only understand cultural differences but to better understand when to leverage them and when to ignore them from the perspective of business strategy. This chapter will ask and answer questions, such as: What are the cross-national differences in the ways individuals gain trust and credibility, communicate, and work together?

The second half of *International Dimensions of Human Resource Management*, Chapters 5 through 7, applies the three foundational areas concurrently when considering the key questions that must be answered within the practice areas of HRM: (1) How do you manage work design and workforce planning globally? (2) How do you manage the competencies of your global talent? and (3) How do you manage their attitudes and behaviors to align with the strategic intent of the organization? Chapter 5 will focus on the way talent is managed in order to accomplish the work necessary for the effective functioning of the organization. As dynamic entities, global organizations must manage the global mobility of their people (e.g. expatriates), the global mobility of jobs (e.g. offshoring) or where to place work, and the global mobility of knowledge (e.g. transnational teams).

Once the work is planned and designed globally to align with strategy, and the context for that work is understood from a comparative and cross-cultural perspective, the next step of the framework would be to effectively manage the competencies, attitudes, and behaviors of the global talent. Chapter 6 will focus on managing the competencies of the global workforce (e.g. recruitment, selection, training, and development) and Chapter 7 will focus on managing their attitudes and behaviors (e.g. compensation and motivation). In both chapters we highlight a few of the cross-national and comparative issues to help raise awareness of the breadth of challenges when making human talent decisions in various countries around the world. Following this, each of these two chapters includes a segment on managing international assignees. We opted to include a larger segment on international assignees in both chapters because, as a group, international assignees' competencies, attitudes, and behaviors can greatly influence a firm's competitiveness around the world. International assignees are, as they should be, generally managed in a way which reflects the high level of influence they can have globally.

The book was not intended to be fully comprehensive – covering every possibly country-specific factor one may encounter for any given country, for every type of organization with their diverse competitive needs, etc. The goal of the book is to raise awareness of the contingencies that must be considered when managing talent globally and decisions to be made on how to apply them. This book is more practical than academic in its treatment of the key issues but does rely on both the academic and practitioner-oriented approaches to describe the conceptual issues. Each chapter will conclude with summary points that will help reiterate the key concepts covered in the respective chapters. We hope the book provides you with an introduction to the many interesting challenges and intriguing complexities of managing the global workforce.

Notes

1 While the academic literature in the area of international business strategy will differentiate among the terms "global", "multinational", and "international" to describe different transnational strategies, the lack of consistency in their use in the literature is unnecessarily confusing for the ideas discussed in this book. This book will use these three terms synonymously to describe all firms, companies, businesses or organizations operating in one or more countries.

2 Adler, N.J. (1983). Cross-cultural Management Issues to be faced. *International Studies of Management and Organization* 13(1–2): 7–45.

3 Bartlett, C. A., and Ghoshal, S. (1987). Managing across borders: New strategic requirements. *Sloan Management Review*, Summer, 7–17. Bartlett, C. A., and Ghoshal, S. (1988) Organizing for worldwide effectiveness: The transnational solution. *California Management Review* 31: 54–74.

4 Prahalad, C. K., and Doz, Y. L. *The Multinational Mission* (New York, NY: The Free Press, 1987).

CHAPTER 2

Global Business Strategy

The Foundation for Managing the Global Workforce

2.1 Lincoln Electric: An Illustrative Example

Lincoln Electric is a manufacturer of welding machinery and consumables which was founded in Cleveland, Ohio in the late 1800s. The founders were fervent believers in individual initiative and equality between workers and managers. They instituted a system of work based on the use of incentives and other complementary practices (e.g. stable employment, an open-door policy, limited benefits). The system worked very well and enabled them to become a leader in the industry. The company attributed so much importance to their work method that, during World War II, they offered to teach it and disseminate it so that it could increase the productivity of North American industry. And it was exactly this method that allowed Lincoln Electric to achieve excellence among US companies throughout its history, surpassing competitors as powerful as Westinghouse.[1]

The success and distinguished history of Lincoln Electric in the US is much less brilliant, however, when we analyze the company's international activities. Although it has achieved some successes in this arena (e.g. in Australia and Canada), Lincoln's work methods encountered many difficulties and conspicuous failures in environments as disparate as Japan, Germany, and Venezuela, where the poor results forced them to close their factories in the 1990s. The enterprise also discovered that operating in the international market-place is different from doing so domestically, and that what worked well at home did not always bring equally good results abroad.

Lincoln's experience is not unique, nor unusual. On the contrary, in many ways, this could also be the story of your company if you were working internationally (or if you were looking to do so). There would be times when going international would not involve problems of personnel, as would be the case if your corporation limited itself to exporting or to buying the services of another company without involving itself in its operations. But there is a greater probability that, as occurred with Lincoln, internationalization would raise many issues and questions in terms of the most efficient ways to manage human resources: How can we gain a competitive advantage in terms of our workers when we operate internationally? What tasks and strategic decisions will we have to adopt? Will we need to use the same (or a similar) system of managing workers throughout the company's international structure? What strategy will we adopt in this arena, and what barriers or difficulties will stand in the way of its implementation? What can we do to facilitate cooperation and exchange of experiences among our foreign subsidiaries?

These are the types of questions that will be discussed in this chapter. We will begin by identifying the fundamental principles upon which a competitive advantage is built when based on individuals in a purely national arena; we will then analyze what changes when we move into an international environment. We will then discuss the strategies and basic capabilities that multinational organizations need to develop in order to succeed and, in turn, manage their human resources globally. Finally, we will identify some principles for aligning human resource practices with a firm's global strategy.

2.2　Principles of Human Resource Management in Multinational Firms

To be successful, companies need to manage their global workforce in ways that fit their strategic needs and the demands of the countries where they operate. Given this, a key question we need to think about is: How to manage a workforce within an organization made up of geographically dispersed business units with different external environments and different skills and capabilities? How, in other words, should we manage talent globally? Successful multinational firms do not harbor any doubts about the importance of this question, and they understand very well the essential role of human resources and its management in making their organizations competitive. They are also aware, however, that managing a global workforce effectively is easier said than done.

The importance of *international human resources* can be seen not only in what the leaders of global firms say (the famous "our people are our greatest resource"), but also in what they do and the time and resources invested in developing policies, systems, and practices to effectively manage people globally. It is now customary that human resource factors are evaluated within a firm's international strategic decisions, such as in due diligence before an acquisition (e.g. the integration of national cultures, the relative competencies of the host national workforce, the availability of talent in the foreign country).

The investment in international human resources is also evidenced in the training programs designed to help employees from many countries improve their language skills, their effectiveness on multicultural teams, their intercultural communications, and intercultural negotiations, among many others. Similarly, human resource management executives in multinationals are often members of the top management executive teams at headquarters and within the foreign subsidiaries of the global firm. Moreover, the issues related to managing the global workforce are increasingly important for line managers. In many companies today, line managers are evaluated according to how well they attract, develop, motivate, and retain the talent within their reporting unit.[2] As these examples demonstrate, multinational companies are clearly aware of the importance and role of international human resource management as a key factor for global success.

Strategic human resource management is defined as the manner of attracting, motivating, developing, and retaining the talent necessary for an organization to attain its objectives.[3] Let's consider this definition in the context of *multinational organizations*. By "multinationals" we mean simply all those organizations that operate in two or more countries. (We will sometimes use "multinationals" interchangeably with the phrase "global firms" or "international companies.") Multinationals can be large corporations such as Exxon,

General Electric, or Toyota as well as small enterprises with just a single foreign subsidiary or offshoring operations.

Regardless of its size, each branch of a multinational must operate in its respective subsidiary country, adhering to each country's laws, while understanding the local cultural norms and sociopolitical realities for doing business. A firm opting to ignore these differences will be disadvantaged compared to other companies that are better able to understand the differences and adapt, when necessary, to compete for resources, market share, and, of course, talent within the local environment. At the same time, a multinational company is a single entity and its activities must be coordinated, in whatever way coordination is best suited, to enjoy benefits of its global scale and of scope.[4] Global firms are highly complex, with continued concurrent strategic pressures to be both integrated globally and responsive locally. These parallel pressures for global coordination or integration and local responsiveness are at the heart of the challenge when considering global business strategies. No two companies will have identical approaches to the strategic business decisions, or subsequent human resources decisions, along this global versus local continuum.

Related case studies conducted in multinationals that are highly admired and valued by the business community (e.g. those that mention Microsoft or General Electric) show that behind the success of many such companies lie well-managed global human talent and an effective strategic human resource management function. This should not be surprising, however, as a multitude of empirical studies have demonstrated the value of human capital and its impact on business outcomes. The authors who have led in this area of research, Brian Becker and Mark Huselid, summed up their findings by saying that based on four national surveys and observations on more than 2000 firms, their judgment is that the effect of a one standard deviation change in the company's high-performance HR system will increase 10–20 % of a firm's market value.[5] Better management of human resources, in other words, yields a better bottom line.

If we try to identify commonalities among the organizations that base their success on human resources, we may be tempted to look for a list of "best practices" (i.e. a specific manner of attracting, retaining, and motivating employees) that are present in all these firms. These efforts, however, often lead to frustration because the human resource management practices that work very well for some firms, and are key to their success, are ineffective in others. For example, in the 1990s, when Microsoft was rising to its zenith, it made a strong point of engaging in excellent human resource practices, such as recruiting from top universities, establishing powerful systems of monetary incentives, promoting competition through the use of employee comparison rating methods, and striving for continuous learning by means of novel and innovative projects.[6] These human resource practices, however, are not the dominant practices found at Intel, even though human resource management was also an essential factor in Intel's success. With a different focus from Microsoft, Intel put its emphasis on human resource practices such as management by objectives, structured problem solving, and running meetings efficiently.[7]

If not specific best practices, per se, what then defines effective human resource management? While differing in strategic execution, there are several fundamental principles upon which human resource management must be built if an organization aspires to compete, in part, on their outstanding human resources. These principles are simple to formulate, but not so simple to follow or convert into a potential source of competitive advantage. (After all, if they were easy to put into practice, they would be within reach for everyone and consequently would yield few advantages.[8]) Some of these principles are shared among firms (irrespective of whether they have any foreign subsidiaries), but others are specific to firms operating globally. Let's begin by analyzing the general principles important for strategic human resources, irrespective of geography.

2.2.1 Principles for Strategic Human Resources

In recent decades much has been written about the strategic value of human talent, of the need to manage this talent with strategic human resource practices. Although it is not easy to draw a unified doctrine from all of this literature, it is possible to identify a series of principles or recommendations in which nearly all experts appear to concur and which constitute the fundamental principles of strategic human resource management. These fundamentals are the ones shown in Figure 2.1: involve top management, maximize employee contributions, align practice with the context of the organization,

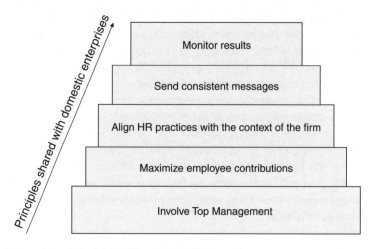

Figure 2.1   Principles of Strategic HRM in MNCs

maintain consistency, and monitor the results. Let's consider each in greater detail.

Involve line managers in managing human talent. Supervising individuals effectively is an essential and critical management task. In fact, as managers move up the organizational chart, their most important tasks often revolve around seeing the big picture (or setting a strategic vision), communicating it effectively, and getting their people to align their efforts behind it. The manner in which one seeks to attract, retain, and motivate employees in order to attain the organization's objectives is a job too important to be delegated to one functional area, the human resource function, alone. Line managers need to set vision and influence their human talent to engage their efforts in alignment with that vision – while human resources professionals (and the HR function in general) supply the guidance and tools for line managers to accomplish this goal.[9] Both sides, line managers and HR professionals, need to evaluate how the available human resources facilitate or impede the success of the organization's strategies, as well as acting as an example and model of the behaviors necessary for the organization to succeed.

This principle of shared responsibility is as valid for domestic businesses as it is for international ones. The only difference is that the challenges for line managers and human resources professionals of managing talent globally are far more complex in multinational firms, given that they need to include a wider variety of employees (e.g. headquarters employees, host country or local employees, expatriates or international assignees), a wider variety of practices (e.g. HR practices developed by headquarters and by subsidiaries), more diverse stakeholders (e.g. headquarters' leaders, subsidiaries' leaders, host country or local employees, national governments), additional situational factors (e.g. culture, legislation, logistics) and, as we will see in the remainder of this chapter, additional objectives and principles. This greater complexity must be taken into consideration when planning how line managers and HR professionals will manage the corporation's global talent.

Maximize employee contributions. As the previous principle suggests, supervising individuals is an essential task of all line management, guided by human resource professionals. Which activities and decisions represent the core of how managers and HR professionals need to manage talent strategically? The *essential HR activities and decisions* have been classified into three categories:[10]

1 Deciding which tasks need to be done and ensuring that the employees are where they need to be when they need to be there;
2 Ensuring that the employees have the requisite competencies to execute these tasks successfully; and
3 Motivating employees so that they utilize their competencies in a productive manner.

These three decisions and subsequent HR activities need to be managed in a way that will maximize employee contributions so that the organization can attain a competitive advantage. From these three activities, it follows that the task of managing talent is not limited to merely attracting talent. In fact, recent studies have shown that the "star" workers (i.e. individuals with exceptional talent), when they move to another organization, make a much more modest contribution than the hiring organization had hoped when they attracted the star in the first place.[11] The contributions of individuals do not depend solely on the knowledge, skills, and abilities that they bring to the organization when they are hired, but also (among other things) on the way in which their tasks are assigned, how they are motivated to expend effort, and how their competencies are developed.[12] Managers need to be held responsible for all of these activities with respect to managing their human talent.

In today's competitive environment, a worthwhile employee contribution consists of doing "something more than standard work from day to day." That is, employees contribute when they are doing things that achieve a higher level of performance and effort, that bring out the best in the organization, and that are flexible. Unfortunately, if we give employees merely ordinary working conditions, we should not expect to get from them extraordinary contributions. Therefore, if we want to fully leverage the contribution and talents of our employees we need to invest more in them: provide them with better training, opportunities for development, better compensation and incentives, and so forth. In short, the organization needs to implement a *norm of reciprocity*,[13] which is a social norm according to which those whom we treat well will respond in kind. Under this norm, individuals realize a maximum contribution when the organization makes them feel important, when they feel involved, when they are listened to, and when they are given opportunities to improve and to participate in successful projects.[14]

A superior workplace environment is precisely one that is governed by this norm of reciprocity, and this holds true for domestic organizations as well as for multinationals. The only difference is the number and type of components that enter into transactions in each case. For example, in many Latin American countries, women are more committed when they work in multinationals than when they work in domestic firms.[15] This is because multinational employers give them something (i.e. better equality in the workplace) that the domestic Latin American employers deny them; as a result, these women respond with more dedication, engagement, and emotional commitment to their organizations.

Align HR practices with the context of the organization. To maximize employee contributions is a goal to which the organization needs to aspire, but the concrete path to arrive at this goal needs to be dictated by the context of each organization. In Table 2.1 we have compiled several factors which are typically cited in the literature as conditional for HR activities and decisions.

The context factor that has received the most attention in the literature is strategy. Different strategies require different tasks, competencies, behaviors, and performance norms by their employees and HR practices that are well aligned with business strategy are those that promote the desired strategic outcomes. For example, in the 1980s Morgan Stanley accomplished a cultural change to empower

Table 2.1 Context Factors That Affect HR Management

Factor	Basic Questions
Strategy	How does the company hope to achieve a competitive advantage over its competitors?
	What tasks need to be accomplished to secure this advantage?
	What competencies do employees need to possess to carry out these tasks?
	What attitudes and behaviors do they need to have?
Employee Concerns	What is the demographic profile of the staff (e.g. age, education, gender)?
	How diverse is the workforce?
	What do employees expect of the company and of labor relations?
Organization and culture	What is the company's size?
	What is its stage of global growth and how does it plan to grow?
	To what industry does it belong?
	What are the values and beliefs that the employees share – or should they share?
External influences	Legal and institutional framework: What aspects of labor relations are regulated? What is the institutional framework?
	Economic environment: What is the labor market like in terms of qualifications, geographic mobility, age, and other variables?
	Social: What are the sociocultural standards for work, behavioral norms affecting work, and sense of social responsibility?

cooperation between its different business units, a very difficult objective in an industry with highly individualistic values and business units that had been traditionally very autonomous and independent. To facilitate this change, Morgan Stanley identified the capabilities and behavioral norms that it wished to promote in its employees, such as teamwork.[16] What they did next was to revise and align their HR practices with these outcomes, including practices such as placing a high value on the ability to work in teams in their selection processes, instituting peer ratings in their performance evaluations, and linking employee compensation to the organization's results. It is important to note that if instead of wanting to promote cooperation the organization had wanted to find ways to stimulate competition between employees, their HR practices would have needed to be very different.

While important, as we can see in Table 2.1, organizational context is a great deal more than just strategy. Other elements are also important, such as the type of business, the organizational culture, or employee concerns. Just as there is no single collection of best practices that work for all firms, there is no single set of contextual issues that apply in the same way across all organizations.[17] Based on contextual issues that may differ across subsidiaries, the type and criteria of evaluation deemed adequate for the manager of one subsidiary in an unexplored market have no reason to be the same as the appropriate way of evaluating another manager whose subsidiary is well developed. Moreover, the most appropriate method of managing employees is also determined by elements of the external context, such as legislation, the labor market, and the political and sociocultural systems where the organization does business.

Context does matter and, as we will see in the next two chapters, may matter tremendously in determining the best configuration of HR practices for any given subsidiary. For example, if we compare the European environment to that of the United States, we will find that in Europe management is generally more limited by interventionist legislation in areas as disparate as hiring, dismissals, training, and trade union negotiations.[18] In sum, HR activities and initiatives need to be adapted to the particular conditions or context of each business unit within each foreign subsidiary. Chapter 3 will offer greater detail about the influence of country-level HR systems on the context of configuring HR practices.

Send consistent messages to employees. HR practices are not only instruments for improving productivity, but also a way of sending messages to employees about what is expected of them. It is important for such messages to be clear and unequivocal, which means that HR practices need to be consistent.[19] For example, there is little value in selecting candidates who possess a great deal of creativity if the positions for which they are to be hired do not involve much autonomy, or if their performance will be evaluated according to systems strongly based on strict adherence to company procedures. On the one hand, we are saying that we value employees who break the mold, while on the other we are asking them to adhere to everything the company stipulates. So that one practice will have the desired consequences, it is necessary for the desired behaviors to be seen as reinforced simultaneously by other practices. This is what we call "internal consistency among practices".[20]

It is important to note, however, that consistency is a difficult goal to achieve in multinational companies, given the multiple contexts. Given that there are so many situational factors (see Table 2.1), it may well be that certain practices, even though they are desired and deemed to send consistent messages, cannot be implemented in some subsidiaries. For example, German law prohibits piecework wages; this made it impossible for Lincoln Electric to transfer this practice to its German subsidiary, forcing a break of internal consistency.

It is also especially difficult in multinationals to maintain *among-employee consistency*, a concept referring to the extent to which different groups of employees are treated in a similar manner.[21] For example, the generous incentives designed to help attract people to accept international assignments and to create a sense of fairness among international employees may have an unfortunate side effect of creating large pay gaps between expatriates and equally qualified local employees.[22] Paying local national employees less may damage their perceptions of the company's procedural and distributive justice. Creating perceptions of fairness among one group of employees (the international assignees) may lead to unfairness perceptions in another group of employees (host nationals who are working with international assignees). As research has repeatedly shown, the benefits of superior HR management do not come from specific practices, but from an integrated and consistent system of practice.

Monitor the results of HR practices. The final principle of good human resource management practices includes regular evaluation of whether the way in which the firm is attracting, developing, and motivating individuals is actually contributing to maximizing employee contributions and improving the organization's performance. Instruments like the "HR Balanced Scorecard"[23] can be helpful in this endeavor. The balanced scorecard uses an integrated system of metrics that allow us to see how the different HR interventions can contribute to building the competencies essential to the organization as well as to attaining the business objectives it has established.

On this point, however, we need to explain two important caveats. The first is that the desired results of implementing HRM practices are usually attainable only over a relatively long time horizon. For example, building a relationship of trust with workers is highly desirable for both labor and management, but this level of trust is not created overnight. Only after it is proven to employees over time that they are respected and that their rights and interests are safeguarded can we hope for a sentiment of pride and an emotional bond to grow in them that will lead them to maximize their contributions to the employer.

The second caveat is that we must not forget that striving for corporate efficiency at any cost is a mistake. Corporate social responsibility with employees stipulates that the goals of the organization are not to be reached at the cost of sacrificing the goals of individuals. This is an important caveat not only for ethical reasons, but also for reasons of company self-interest. In a recent investigation in France, for example, researchers found that 70% of individual investors would be disposed to sell their assets if the firm in which they had invested committed a serious violation of labor laws, as they would judge the firm to be lacking in corporate social responsibility.[24]

The probability of winning the loyalty of customers, generating profits, and attracting good candidates in the labor market is superior for an organization that has a reputation for treating its employees ethically compared to an organization that has been involved in various scandals or that treats its employees in an opportunistic and instrumental fashion. Hence, guarding the "corporate reputation" by, in part, treating all employees ethically is important globally. This is especially important in the case of multinational corporations, which are usually subjected to more scrutiny across a diversity of ethical norms coupled with a greater need to be sensitive to multiple governmental concerns, labor relations, cultural norms of fairness, and the like.[25] Designing and implementing human resource management practices that can meet the principles above while contributing decisively to the company's competitive advantage is a challenge for companies operating both domestically and those operating in multiple countries around the world.

2.2.2   Principles for Global Human Resource Management

In order to achieve the alignment of strategic human resource management practices with the goals of a multinational firm, it is important to understand the strategic capabilities most multinational firms seek as they expand and compete globally. In an influential study, Christopher Bartlett and Sumantra Ghoshal[26] examined companies like Cadbury, IBM, Hewlett-Packard, Shell, Philips, and Citibank and found that the most successful multinationals developed three basic cross-national capabilities simultaneously. The first is *local responsiveness*: multinational firms should carry out an exhaustive analysis and investigation of markets and differentiate their products to fit the preferences of their clients, the characteristics of the sector, and the cultural and legal environment of each of the national markets where they operate. The second capability is *global integration* of the firm's operations in order to take advantage of different national factors of production, to leverage economies of scale in all activities, and to share costs and investments across different markets and business units. The third capability is developing *innovation and a learning organization*, which requires that the different units (the center or subsidiaries) learn from each other and exchange innovations in management systems and processes. These three cross-national capabilities that Bartlett and Ghoshal identified are considered at a more general strategic level, but they can serve as a reference from which developing HR practices should follow. These strategic cross-national capabilities (local responsiveness, global integration, and worldwide innovation and learning) serve as a backdrop for developing strategic decisions when managing talent in multinational firms.

Let us imagine a business that is about to open a foreign subsidiary. Undoubtedly, there will be many issues that need to be decided: what mode of entry to utilize, how to finance the operation, how to compete, what kind of commercial tools to develop, and so forth. But what interests us is the system that the organization will need to use in the new subsidiary to attract, retain, develop, and motivate employees. To answer this question, there are only three possibilities: try to replicate the parent company's system in the subsidiary, design a totally new system, or find an intermediate solution (e.g. exporting some of the parent company's practices and adapting others). These three options correspond to the three basic strategies of international HRM identified in the literature: exporting, adapting, and integrating.[27] We will examine each one in greater detail and determine which is the most appropriate.

Multinational "exporters" endeavor to transplant their HR systems from the parent company to the subsidiary. Their belief is that the parent company's way of doing things is superior or more appropriate than other systems. They are striving for global efficiency – exporting their system may help ensure high standardization across various subsidiary locations. If the firm encounters problems in applying a given HR practice in a foreign location (as evidenced by decreased productivity, increased turnover, or the inability to recruit qualified personnel), the problem is likely to be attributed to a problem with the foreign location (as opposed to a problem with the headquarters-based practice). Lincoln Electric serves as an example of this exporter approach. The company tried to establish its famous system of incentives in many different environments, only to find that in many of them it did not work. The blame was placed on foreign cultures, as the company president, Donald F. Hastings, publicly affirmed in a 1997 interview:

> We had an incentive program that was based in the belief that everybody in the world would be willing to work a little harder to enhance their lives and their families and their incomes. It was an erroneous assumption.[28]

Unlike exporters, *multinational "adapters"* follow the logic that there is no such thing as "one best way" and the best approach to managing people globally is to develop distinct systems for different locations around the globe. Fueling this perspective are well-noted failed attempts at exporting HR practices, such as the use of management by objectives in France,[29] participative decision making in Russia,[30] or an open door policy in Italy.[31]

While adapters do not serve as a strong approach for global efficiency with HR practices, they are potentially quite effective in the pursuit of local responsiveness. Firms with this approach adapt their HR systems to local norms for how to manage as well as other aspects of the local sociocultural context. As the saying goes, "when in Rome do as the Romans do." According to this logic, HRM practices are typically decentralized from the parent to the various locations with scarce guidelines from headquarters so that the various subsidiaries are allowed to have different HR systems and practices. Several well-known companies have been quite successful with this approach.

For example, until the 1980s firms like IBM and Procter & Gamble followed a consistent strategy of creating a mini-IBM or mini-P&G in each of the markets where they operated, and adapting everything necessary to function efficiently in those markets.[32]

Multinational "integrators" develop a dual HR strategy. On the one hand, they strive to maintain a certain internal consistency among subsidiaries by standardizing some of their management practices. At the same time, however, they try to decentralize other practices in order to adapt to the local environment, at least to a small extent. A good example of this is Unilever's program of *Best Proven Practice*, which permits especially successful practices to be applied in all of the company's plants, regardless of where a given practice originated. Similarly, career development in the major multinational auditing firms (e.g. PricewaterhouseCoopers, Ernst & Young) defined by an "Up or Out" promotion system through a specific series of levels (junior auditor, senior auditor, manager, partner) has been implemented throughout the international network of these organizations, even though they adapt other elements of their human resource systems (e.g. content of training courses, vacations) to the sociocultural context where each of their subsidiaries operate.

Given these three options, a logical question is: Which approach is best? Unfortunately, there is no single best approach. Rather, each approach has to be assessed on a case-by-case basis and on a practice-by-practice basis. To assess when to apply which approach, it is necessary to identify the strategic HR capacities of the firm and to evaluate in what way HR practices will facilitate their success and development. As shown in Figure 2.2, global human resource management in a multinational corporation requires adherence to the following six principles. The way in which they do so, however, is determined by their strategy. Let's consider the following.

1 **Integrate and optimize tasks and activities globally.** In contrast to the policy of creating mini-replicas of the parent company in foreign countries, firms may benefit from capitalizing on differences present in the local labor markets in terms of competence, capabilities, wages, and the like that will allow them to locate parts of the organization's value chain in the countries with the most advantageous conditions.[33] This explains, for example, the existence of call centers in India, factories in China, and centers of Research and Development (R&D) in Western Europe.

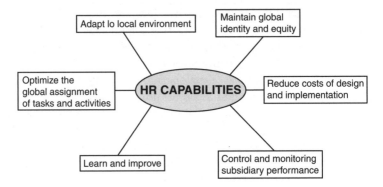

Figure 2.2 International HR Capabilities

Collectively, diverse subsidiaries in India, China, and Western Europe can optimize the firm's overall tasks and activities.

2 **Adapt to the local environment, as needed.** Because of differences in country HR systems, multinational firms need to be flexible in their company's human resource practices in order to attract, retain, and motivate staff in the manner most appropriate to the local market. Failure to do so may violate local labor laws or potentially lose the competitive advantage by damaging the firm's employer reputation through culturally inappropriate human resources practices.

3 **Retain core values globally.** Although it is made up of multiple subsidiaries, a multinational corporation is also a single business entity. Even when it desires to adapt to local conditions to attract and retain employees, it may need to act in a way that is counter to the cultural values of a particular location to adhere to the core values of the organization. For example, it would be wrong (and potentially damaging to a firm's global reputation) to not promote women to managerial positions just because "machismo" and discrimination against women are widespread in certain countries' local environments. Some values are core to the company and should be maintained globally, while some may be free to vary.

4 **Control and monitor the performance of the various subsidiaries on common metrics.** How can one compare the respective performance of employees who are evaluated according to totally different systems and criteria? If different units

function with different practices and approaches, it is difficult to compare them on common metrics. However, a common performance management system is critical within a multinational to ensure important comparisons across units. One implication, however, is that this act of monitoring results across subsidiaries has a tendency to create pressure toward standardization across subsidiaries over time.

5 **Reduce costs of design and implementation of HR practices.** Multinationals enjoy benefits of scale and scope in HR just as in other functional areas. Adapting HR practices to local environments increases the costs of design and implementation.[34] The costs incurred in developing an HR information system for a given subsidiary, for example, can be amortized if it is also created for use at the implemented and at the corporate level. If each subsidiary functions with different management practices, the global costs will be higher than if an attempt is made to share or distribute the same practices among various subsidiaries. Wherever possible and practical, global firms should try to extend their economies of scale to HR systems and practices.

6 **Learn from the subsidiaries and improve the company.** Diversity is one advantage which multinational firms have over purely local or domestic firms. Given that foreign subsidiaries operate in different surroundings and countries, they are exposed to a variety of experiences and practices, some of which can also be useful in other countries. Each unit of the organization can be a source of abilities, capabilities, knowledge, and innovation. However, multinational businesses must be capable of leveraging this advantage and facilitating the transfer of best practices among their affiliates.[35] Only by doing so can they realize and empower their knowledge base and continue improving over the long term.

As these six principles demonstrate, there are different factors that multinational corporations have to consider when developing their HR systems for the organization and their subsidiaries. A key challenge, however, is that some of these factors act as forces for standardization across subsidiaries while others exert pressure toward differentiation in how subsidiaries are managed. As a result, they directly impact the relative effectiveness of each of the HR strategies of exporting, adapting, and integrating.

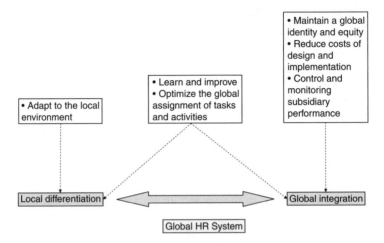

Figure 2.3　A Dual Logic

Some of the principles mentioned above apply pressure on organizations in completely opposite directions (see Figure 2.3). If we focus on the firm's capability of adapting to the local environment, for example, it is logical to design a unique method of attracting, retaining and motivating employees that is adjusted to the idiosyncratic values of each location where the organization does business. If, however, the firm aspires to greater global corporate coordination and cost efficiency, it will be logical to integrate and standardize its HR system. A focus on learning and innovating requires both differentiation (so that there will be variety in the things to be learned) and integration (so that various subsidiaries transfer and benefit from each other's good experiences).

As you might expect, each of these approaches centers on some of the abovementioned principles at the expense of the others. For example, the adaptive approach aims to maximize local adaptation but ignores other, equally important decisions (global control and equity, cost containment, etc.). Similarly, for the sake of global identity and cost efficiency, the exporter approach capitalizes on the benefits of standardizing the human resource system. At the same time, however, a complete focus on standardization would likely impede not only local responsiveness but also the ability to realize the benefits of learning and improving.

Considering all the advantages and disadvantages, the integrated approach appears to be the most desirable as it aims to achieve all of the central HR capabilities simultaneously. This goal, however, and the manner in which the capabilities put pressure on the organization in opposing directions (differentiation versus integration), need to be conceived as a continual challenge in terms of *preserving variety and local adaptation* while simultaneously *establishing a foundation for global integration and knowledge transfer*.[36] While this strategy has great promise and is the most likely approach to adhere to the six principles noted above, this integrated strategy toward HR practices is also the most complex.

Existing evidence suggests that companies realize the potential for this approach and strive to implement it, in part, across some HR practices, rather than adopting a pure exporter or adapter approach. For example, in a study of six HR practices (vacations, benefits, executive bonuses, participation in decision making, gender composition of executive teams, and the quantity of training received) in North American subsidiaries of different multinationals, multinational companies did not all adapt (or standardize) to the same extent.[37] While some practices were usually very much adapted (i.e. vacations, gender composition of executive teams, or benefits), others tended to replicate what existed in headquarters or other business units (e.g. bonuses, level of decision making participation).

2.3   Strategic Global Human Resource Management

To be strategic as we manage the global workforce, we consider the way HR practices are developed globally. Firms operating globally will need to (1) decide which HR practices to implement in accordance with local norms and customers and which to standardize and (2) foster learning and cooperation across business units and subsidiaries around the world. Both will be explored in greater detail below.

2.3.1   *Decide Which HR Practices to Adapt and Which to Standardize*

Which HR practices should be adapted to local conditions and which ones should be standardized? The answer, in part, depends on the organization and how it is trying to compete globally. There are, however, some trends across firms. In general, there are three factors that are relevant for considering which HR practices to localize.

- **Localize practices if something is legislated.** One general trend is that practices that tend to be adapted are those that are strongly regulated. Legislation obliges organizations to follow certain procedures. For example, in Germany companies are obligated to give a minimum of 24 paid vacation days. It is important to note that it is not easy to find German-owned businesses in the United States that give as many paid vacation days as the law requires in Germany. The German-owned firms have adapted to the American norm of fewer vacation days.
- **Localize practices if a given social norm is exceptionally strong.** In some cases there may be a cultural value so deeply embedded that to try to override it might generate negative publicity or simply might be too difficult and generally not worth the added work. Those things that are subject to strong expectations or social conventions (but not core to a strategic initiative) are often adapted, obligating the organization to behave in a more local way. For example, in some manufacturing facilities in the Middle East, it is easier to ask a husband's permission to allow a female employee to work – or to segregate male from female employees – than it is to try to override the cultural norm regarding the role of women. Some cultural battles are not worth fighting in the name of consistency.
- **Localize practices if a given social norm affects a non-strategic practice.** Some HR practices that are adapted are those that are considered least important from a strategic viewpoint. When Unilever took over Ben & Jerry's (an ice cream manufacturer known for corporate social responsibility), they stumbled upon a company where costumes were worn to celebrate Halloween. As the costumes did not interfere with the strategic goals of the firm, Dutch Unilever had no reason to change the practice (nor did it have any reason to extend the practice to other subsidiaries).

As these three principles indicate, there are certain factors that provide incentives for multinationals to localize practices. At the same time, however, there are also some factors that exert pressure to standardize practices across subsidiary locations. With some HR practices, the parent company generally has more interest in controlling (and, in general, standardizing) differences so practices are uniform around the world. There are two factors that are relevant for considering which HR practices to standardize.

- **Standardize HR practices essential for competitive advantage.** Some HR practices are too important for the firm to allow for local variation. For example, a study of management practices in Japanese-owned subsidiaries in the United States[38] revealed that the fundamental source of competitive advantage of these businesses in Japan resided in their ability to turn out products of superior quality with zero defects, and that certain HR practices, such as job rotation, on-the-job training, teamwork, and cooperative labor–management relations, were essential for achieving such advantage. Consequently, the Japanese firms organized work in their North American subsidiaries consistent with these HR practices. In contrast, other practices which were perceived as less central, such as wearing uniforms or having all employees eat in the same cafeteria, while typical at headquarters, were not implemented in every subsidiary.
- **Standardize HR practices affecting the key employees in the most critical roles.** Not all employees are equally valuable in terms of generating a competitive advantage.[39] Organizations usually exercise more control (and, therefore, standardize their practices to a greater extent) over the group of employees that it considers the most critical who occupy the firm's wealth-creating roles. Brand managers in a consumer goods firm or research scientists in a pharmaceutical company are two examples of employees in key roles. Continuing with the Japanese example, many Japanese corporations consider those who are in assembly or operations roles to be essential to the firm's performance, so they export their HR policies to retain control over this group of employees, while at the same time they allow more local policies for their managers.

While these points provide some factors that tend to encourage multinationals to simultaneously localize some HR practices while standardizing others, it is possible that conflicting interests among these might exist. For example, what should you do if, because of its strategic importance, you want to standardize a practice that clashes with the local culture or environment? Rather than changing the practices to fit in with the local environment, a hybrid response might be to place a person in the location who adheres to corporate values (a tactic we will discuss in more detail in Chapter 3) while allowing the practice to remain localized. This is one strong reason why companies use expatriates – to replicate their corporate culture or strategies in another location.

Businesses like Accenture or McKinsey do not seek to hire local individuals who are "typical" or culturally representative of their foreign subsidiary's locale, but instead they seek out individuals who can adapt and adjust well globally to the corporation's work methods and values. Since these HR practices, over time, have provided Accenture and McKinsey with a competitive advantage globally, they have a very strong reason to continue the practice of hiring those individuals who are atypical of their culture.

2.3.2 Increase Cooperation and Learning among Subsidiaries

As part of the broader global firm, it is important that, even with a strong local sensibility, the multinational corporation be able to foster a degree of cooperation among employees across the subsidiaries. This is particularly important for companies competing on a strategy of learning and innovation. It is possible that some particularly effective HR practices developed in one subsidiary might be useful if shared with or transferred to other subsidiaries.

To transfer HR practices, the firm must take an activity or management initiative (e.g. a training program, a method of incentives, a performance evaluation system, or a selection instrument) that is carried out in a superior manner in some part of the multinational (the source unit) and replicate it in another unit (the recipient unit) that either lacks it or is carrying it out poorly. For example, the headquarters of Renault in France developed a complex and sophisticated system of measuring internal customer satisfaction with the services provided by departments serving internal customers; this system was perfectly usable (with small modifications) in all of Renault's subsidiaries, which promoted its transfer and standardization. The internal transfer of practices, however, had no reason to be limited to those that occurred between the parent company and its foreign subsidiaries, as the example may suggest, but instead could occur in all directions within the multinational. The system of incentives that exists at the headquarters of Endesa, an energy and power generation company based in Spain, was replicated from the one existing in its subsidiary in Chile. In this case, the HR practice moved from a foreign subsidiary to headquarters.

Some HR practices can be very useful in one specific business unit of a firm but of little value or interest elsewhere. For example, in cultures such as Germany where punctuality is expected, job candidates will show up on time for interviews as a general cultural norm with little differentiation. In Costa Rica, however, a culture where punctuality is not an expected norm, candidates who arrive on time for their interviews are rated very positively. This punctuality test may differentiate those who are highly motivated for the job in Costa Rica but it may not differentiate them at all in Germany. Moreover, transferring best practices is far from easy. Gabriel Szulanski developed the concept of "internal stickiness" to refer to the difficulty of transferring knowledge within organizations. He identifies four sets of factors influencing the difficulty of knowledge transfer:

- characteristics of the knowledge transferred (i.e. the knowledge is ambiguous or unclear or unproven);
- characteristics of the source (i.e. the transferor has a lack of motivation or is not perceived as reliable);
- characteristics of the recipient (i.e. the recipient of knowledge has a lack of motivation or does not have absorptive capacity [an ability to adapt the information to their circumstances]); and
- characteristics of the context in which the transfer takes place (i.e., barren organizational context or arduous relationship).

In an empirical study, he found that the major barriers to internal knowledge transfer are the recipient's lack of absorptive capacity, knowledge ambiguity, and an arduous relationship between the source and the recipient.

Another barrier for knowledge transfer is offered by Tatiana Kostova who proposed an alternative set of factors affecting the success of transfers of knowledge. Some factors are social and involve the degree to which the regulatory, cognitive, and normative profiles of the home country and the recipient country are similar or different. Other factors are organizational in nature and involve compatibility between the values implied by the knowledge transferred and the values underlying the unit's organizational culture, or the degree to which the unit's organizational culture is supportive of learning, chance, and innovation. Finally, other potential barriers that were noted are individual in nature, referring to the attitudes of individuals regarding their commitment to, identification with, and trust in the parent company.

There are times when multinational corporations strive to share knowledge across subsidiaries to help improve other subsidiaries and the multinational corporation as a whole. However, there are a host of potential barriers that may exist to prevent this from happening as effectively as possible. The example of Lincoln Electric, with which we opened this chapter, can serve as an illustration of these potential barriers.

2.4   Returning to Lincoln Electric

At the beginning of this chapter we discussed Lincoln Electric and noted that Lincoln has been a highly successful business in the United States that encountered some challenges in reproducing its success abroad. In particular, the company's strong drive toward international expansion, which took place between 1988 and 1994 under the presidency of George Willis, encountered many difficulties. During this period the company acquired plants in several new countries (Germany, Ireland, Italy, the Netherlands, Norway, Spain, the United Kingdom, Brazil, and Mexico) and built new plants in Japan and Venezuela. In 1993 they found that these new plants, especially the ones in Europe, were dragging the entire corporation down. For the first time in its history, Lincoln declared a financial loss.

Using the Szulanski model mentioned above, we can see the principal barriers and difficulties that prevented the successful transfer of Lincoln Electric's system of incentives; these are shown in Figure 2.4. Such barriers are classified by whether they pertain to context, source of transfer, recipient, or to the particular practice being transferred.

Among the barriers pertaining to context, it is worth mentioning that the economic environment was unfavorable. During the period

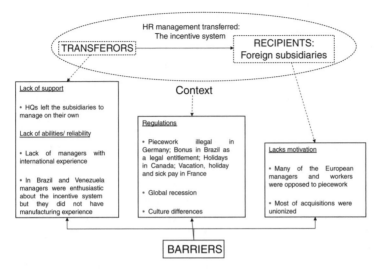

Figure 2.4 Lincoln Electric: An Illustrative Example

when the majority of the company's expansion took place there was a global recession. This impeded workers' perceptions of the benefits of a system that linked effort with compensation. The differences in legal environments also presented serious obstacles. In Brazil each bonus paid in two consecutive years is automatically converted into something to which the employee has a legal right; in France the law requires paid vacations and sick leave, a practice the company had avoided in the US, where they had a policy of limiting worker benefits. Finally, and as affirmed by Willis's successor Don Hastings, cultural differences also caused many difficulties. Things that were effective motivators for Americans were not motivating for Germans, Spaniards, or Japanese. Instead of selecting employees who were a good fit with the company's work systems, Lincoln had inherited a number of employees with a system of values that clashed with those the company espoused.

Other barriers arose from the work system. In the first place, the company did not provide the necessary support. Lincoln's corporate culture was so strongly oriented toward individualism that the company adopted a "sink or swim" attitude toward its subsidiaries, leaving them to administer themselves to a great extent. This contrasted with top management's strong support for the characteristic work system in the USA (Cleveland). In the second place, the transferors or implementers of the system lacked the necessary competencies. The headquarters in Cleveland did not provide managers with significant international experience. The implementation of the system of incentives was left to the managers of the acquired businesses. In some subsidiaries, such as Venezuela and Brazil, the company had replaced the legacy managers with Lincoln distributors who were enthusiastic about Lincoln's work system, but who had no experience in manufacturing; the headquarters managers from Cleveland gave them very little assistance.

There were also barriers arising from the recipients of the system. The majority of Lincoln's acquisitions were unionized, and in each of these labor–management relations were less cordial than in Lincoln. Therefore, the trust relationship that is essential for the system to function was lacking. Moreover, many of the European managers and workers were philosophically opposed to the use of individual incentives, and they appeared to value vacation time more than the extra income they received from bonuses.

Finally, there may very well have been barriers within the system being transferred: piecework. Research has made it clear that piecework only functions under very specific conditions. For example, workers' activities must be so self-contained that they can work at their own pace; they should not entail many different tasks, some of them easier to measure than others; and workers should not be affected by factors beyond their control. All of these conditions existed in Cleveland, where the work was organized in a modular way. However, when many of the subsidiaries were acquired they did not thoroughly analyze how compatible their work design was with Lincoln's system of incentives.

What is demonstrated in the case of Lincoln Electric is that the global management of HR systems is plagued with difficulties and barriers. Some companies who have confronted similar problems have been able to effectively implement HR practices and systems that have helped them attain a position of international leadership. At the same time, many companies have failed. Business schools are full of success stories, as well as failures in international HRM. Another key point is that these barriers highlight the difficulties associated with navigating country HR systems and cultural differences around the globe. In light of these challenges, the next two chapters are devoted to these specific issues.

2.5 Chapter Conclusions

This foundational chapter discussed human resource management principles generally. Then we considered international HRM in the context of global business strategies and capabilities that multinational organizations need to develop in order to succeed. The alignment of human resource practices with a firm's global strategy was also discussed as we drew the following conclusions:

Be aware of complexity. Multiculturalism and geographical dispersion contribute to making operations more complex in the international arena. Managing the global workforce involves managing a wider group of employees (e.g. employees at headquarters, local employees, expatriates), a greater diversity of practices (e.g. HR practices at headquarters and different subsidiaries), a greater number of stakeholders (e.g. headquarters, international assignees, local employees, government), and more situational factors (e.g. culture, legislation). Managing a global workforce carries with it additional issues and activities, with respect to the manner of managing cultural differences among subsidiaries and of facilitating cooperation among them and coping with cross-border differences in country HR systems.

Follow the principles that contribute to the success of the HR systems. Although the discontinuities and differences between local management and their international counterparts have been emphasized, it is also true that, in both arenas, one needs, for example, for top management to be involved, for HR practices to contribute to increasing employees' productivity and contributions, or for HR programs to be well adapted to the context of the organization and consistent with one another. Much of what is learned in the domestic environment is also applicable internationally.

Determine which practices you wish to standardize and which you wish to adapt. There are many reasons why it is desirable and efficient to standardize certain management practices. Doing so helps reproduce the organization's competitive advantage in other markets, reduces costs, facilitates control, maintains global equity and identity, and potentially helps corporations profit from the successful experiences of other subsidiaries and transfer what has been learned from them. There are also good strategic reasons to adapt HR practices to the local environment. The challenge for a multinational is to face both of these kinds of pressures simultaneously and to identify how to be simultaneously locally responsive and globally integrated.

Develop an appropriate HR strategy to manage talent. A multinational firm needs to be capable of attracting, retaining, developing, and motivating associates in the manner that is most appropriate to the local market or most consistent with an overall strategy. One way to do this is to decentralize and change the work system in order to design it in accord with local standards. Another way is to maintain the company's system, take the elements of it that are conducive to adaptation and make them flexible, and place strong emphasis on selecting local candidates who are a good fit with the company's way of working. This last option is most appropriate when your work system contributes to a competitive advantage. Another way would be to seek out atypical candidates who do not reflect the values of the local environment but who align more closely with the firm's values.

Create mechanisms for learning and cooperation among HR professionals in subsidiaries and headquarters. The possibility of transferring knowledge, experiences, and best practices among subsidiaries is one of the advantages of multinationals. This needs to be applied in the area of HR as well, and to do so, it is important to create mechanisms that facilitate knowledge transfer in this area. In Chapter 3 we will discuss this in more detail, but globally distributed teams, international assignments, communities of practice, and global expertise networks are examples of such mechanisms. All of these mechanisms permit the organization to create social interaction among those in charge of HR in the different business units and to exchange experiences and knowledge, both formally and informally.

Understand the potential difficulties in transferring HR practices across borders. Transferring HR systems can convey many advantages, but research and international experience have shown that it is not easy. Many barriers can get in the way of success for such transfers. Culture is one of these, but it is not the only one. Lack of support, ability, or motivation on the part of those who are making the transfer, possible rejection on the part of recipients, the economic or legislative context, or the characteristics of the system being transferred are other potential barriers. Anticipating such barriers as much as possible, and examining the methods and initiatives that can prevent or counteract them, is an essential task.

Notes

1   We are simplifying from the original case Lincoln Electric: Venturing Abroad, HBS, No 9-398-095, prepared by Jamie O'Connell. The full case is extremely interesting, and we heartily recommend its reading.

2   A more complete discussion of recent trends in the international HRM area can be seen in Tony Edwards and Chris Rees, *International Human Resource Management: Globalization, National Systems and Multinational Companies* (FT Prentice Hall, 2006).

3   Lepak, D. and Gowan, M., *Human Resource Management* (Prentice Hall, 2008).

4   Nohria, N. and Ghoshal, S., *The Differentiated Network: Organizing Multinational Corporations for Value Creation* (San Francisco: Jossey-Bass, 1997).

5   Becker, B. E. and Huselid, M. A. (1998). High Performance Work Systems and Firm Performance: A synthesis of research and Managerial Implications, *Research in Personnel and Human Resources Journal* 16(1): 53–101.

6   See Microsoft: Competing for Talent, Harvard Business School Cases: 9-300-001.

7   Intel Corp. 1968–2003, Harvard Business School Cases: 703427.

8   Barney, J. B. and Wright, P. (1998). On becoming a strategic partner. The role of human resources in gaining competitive advantage, *Human Resource Management* 37(1): 31–47.

9   Ulrich, D., *Human Resource Champions: The Next Agenda for Adding Value and Delivering Result* (Boston: Harvard Business Review, 1997).

10 Lepak, D. and Gowan, M., *Human Resource Management* (Prentice Hall, 2008).

11 Groysberg, B., McLean, A. N., and Nohria, N. (2006). Are leaders portable?, *Harvard Business Review*, May 2006.

12 Groysberg, B., Nanda, A., and Nohria, N. (2005). The risky business of hiring stars, *Harvard Business Review*, December 2005.

13 A more complete discussion of this norm is found in James Baron and David Kreps, *Strategic Human Resources. Frameworks for General Managers* (New York: John Wiley and Sons, Inc, 1999).

14 Pfeffer, J. (1999). Seven practices of successful organizations, *Health Forum Journal* 42(1): 24–27.

15 Ogliastri, Enrique (2008). "La Cultura Organizacional en America Latina", Seminar at the Incae Business School, Costa Rica.

16 See Burton, M. Diane, The Firmwide 360° Performance Evaluation Process at Morgan Stanley, Harvard Business School Cases 9-498-053 (1998).

17 Newman, K. L. and Nollen, S. D. (1996). Culture and Congruence: The Fit between Management Practices and National Culture, *Journal of International Business Studies* 27(4): 753–779.

18 Brewster, C. (1995). Towards a European Model of Human Resource Management, *Journal of International Business Studies* 26(1): 1–12.

19 Baron and Kreps, n. 13 above.

20 Lepak and Gowan, n. 10 above.

21 Baron and Kreps, n. 13 above.

22 See Chen, C. C., Choi, J., and Chi, S. C. (2002). Making justice sense of local-expatriate compensation disparity: Mitigation by local referents, ideological explanations, and interpersonal sensitivity in China-foreign joint ventures, *Academy of Management Journal* 45(4): 807–826; and Toh, S. M. and DeNisi, A. (2003). Host country national reactions to expatriate pay policies: a model and implications, *Academy of Management Review* 28(4): 606–621.

23 Becker, B. E., Huselid, M. A., and Ulrich, D. (2001). *The HR Scorecard: Linking People, Strategy, and Performance*, Boston, MA: Harvard Business School Publishing.

24 Lipovetski, G., *Metamorfosis de la cultura liberal* (ed. Anagrama, 2002).

25 Adler, N. J. (1983). Cross-cultural Management Issues to be faced, *International Studies of Management and Organization* 13(1–2): 7–45.

26 Bartlett, C. A. and Ghoshal, S. *Managing Across Borders. The Transnational Solution* (Boston, MA: Harvard Business School Press, 1989).

27 Taylor, S., Beechler, S., and Napier, N. (1996). Toward an integrative model of strategic international human resource management, *Academy of Management Review* 21(4): 959–965. A similar typology can be found in Pertmultter, H. (1969) The Tortuous Evolution of the Multinational Corporation, *Columbia Journal of World Business*, January–February: 9–18.

28 Cited in Richard M. Hodgetts, A conversation with Donald F. Hastings of the Lincoln Electric Company, *Organizational Dynamics*, January 1997.

29 Trepo, G. (1973). Management style a la Francaise, *European Business*, Autumn: 71–79.

30 Welsh, D., Luthans, F., and Sommer, S. M. (1993). Managing Russian Factory Workers: The Impact of U.S. Based Behavioral and Participative Techniques. *Academy of Management Journal* 36: 58–79.

31 Laurent, A. (1983). The Cultural Diversity of Western Management Conceptions, *International Studies of Management and Organisation* 8(1–2): 75–96.

32 Pankaj Ghemawat (2007). Managing differences: The central Challenger of Global Strategy, *Harvard Business Review*, March: 2–13.

33 Guemawat, P., n. 32 above.

34 Gómez Mejia, L.R. and Palich, L.E. (1997). Cultural Diversity and the Performance of Multinational Firms, *Journal of International Business Studies* 28(4): 736–758.

35 Nohria and Ghoshal, n. 4 above.
36 Morris, S., Snell, S., and Wright, P., "A resource based view of international human resources: Toward a framework of integrative and creative capabilities", in Gunter K. Stahl and Ingmar Bjorkman, *Handbook of Research in International Human Resources* (Edward Elgar Publishing, 2000).
37 Rosenzweig, S. and Nohria, N. (1994). Influences on Human Resource Management Practices in Multinational Corporations, *Journal of International Business Studies* 25(2): 222–251.
38 Beechler, and Yang, J. Z. (1994). The transfer of Japanese-style management to American subsidiaries: Contingencies, constraints, and competencies. *Journal of International Business Studies* 467–491.
39 Lepak, D. and Snell, S. (1999). The Human Resource Architecture: Toward a theory of human capital allocation and development, *Academy of Management Review* 24(1): 31–48.

CHAPTER 3

Comparative HR Systems

The Context for Managing the Global Workforce

3.1 Lincoln Electric Revisited: An Illustrative Example

After reading the previous chapters you probably now have a more acute awareness that managers must consider how to "think globally" and "act locally" in a balance that is consistent with their global business strategy in order to achieve competitive success. This is easier said than done, however, as our discussion of Lincoln Electric in Chapter 2 illustrates some of the difficulties of trying to expand internationally. Some of these problems might be viewed as relating to lack of support of management in different locations or other strategic concerns. However, a good part of the difficulty faced by Lincoln Electric relates to fundamental differences in how people are managed in different parts of the world, given the countries' respective HR systems. Some of these differences are cultural in nature, but many are systemic factors affecting how people are managed which are embedded in the social, legal, and environmental infrastructure of each country – their country-level HR systems.

Returning to the Lincoln Electric case for illustration, Lincoln's system for compensation and incentives was troublesome in Brazil where bonuses paid in consecutive years are converted into a legal right of pay. This conversion was directly against the intent of the incentive plans that are famous at Lincoln Electric. One of the major benefits of the incentive plan as designed is that it provides a strong incentive, and significant reward, for extensive effort by employees. If that incentive is rolled into base pay, its motivating impact is diminished. In France, as another example from the same case, the required benefits associated with vacation and paid time off were substantially greater than those that the company had provided to its US employees. This resulted in increased costs, a factor that impacts Lincoln's ability to remain a highly efficient operation. The experience of Lincoln Electric highlights the challenges for managing within a transnational context. What might be acceptable, expected, and effective in one country might be illegal, unexpected, or ineffective in another.

The differences across country-level HR systems become increasingly critical as organizations expand internationally, consider locations in other countries, and build and manage a global workforce across subsidiaries. The prospect of managing employees in a foreign subsidiary, for example, is full of HR challenges related to issues such as the supply of labor, who and how to hire, what to pay, how to train and develop, the terms of employment, and the like.

The focus of this chapter is to explore the key HR systems or structural aspects of different countries affecting the management of talent around the world. While organizations certainly make conscious decisions regarding how to strategically manage their talent in different countries, sometimes elements of these decisions are beyond managerial control; they are a function of the HR systems within the given country. When it comes to managing the multinational organization, there are many social, legal, and institutional factors within each country – the country-level HR system – that influence the practice of human resource management (HRM) within each country where global firms operate. They include:[1]

- The competencies of the workforce, influenced by educational systems (e.g. mandatory education, literacy rates, language skills).
- The labor economic systems across countries, including their relative rates of turnover and the level of unemployment.
- The legal and regulatory system governing the practice of HR (especially those affecting the flexibility of the wage bill), including the ability to adjust hours (overtime) and the ability to adjust headcount (layoffs, temporary or contract work) – and other

regulated country-level issues such as the level of state-provided (versus employer-provided) medical and health care.

▪ The state of labor relations and unionization (e.g. works councils) and the level of collaboration with management that is mandated or expected.

▪ The cultural norms (discussed in greater detail in Chapter 4) for work-related values and business in general.

This chapter will focus on the first four of these issues. Chapter 4 will focus on the fifth issue, cultural differences. First, we will consider the implications of the differences in the competencies of workers within countries and how this will affect HR practices within subsidiaries; as countries vary with respect to the types of skills and abilities prevalent among their workers, this variance will affect HR practices such as selection, training, and development. Second, we will consider the differences in economic conditions regarding the labor pool around the world. Some countries experience very high unemployment while others do not, and these differences have direct implications for the supply of available competencies, the ability to staff a given subsidiary, and workforce planning. Third, there are considerable differences regarding regulatory or legal considerations across countries. These differences directly affect what is, and is not, appropriate and/or required for organizations managing people within any given country. These differences may influence a variety of HR practices including work hours, working conditions, compensation, benefits, and many others. Also related to the provision of benefits is whether any given country provides medical or health care to all citizens (or if health care is a benefit sought out by employees). Finally, it is important to recognize that there are differences in labor or industrial relations around the world affecting work design and involvement or collaboration across workers and management. This is the last issue covered in this chapter.

3.2 Cross-Border Differences in Workforce Competence

Multinational organizations depend on people throughout the world to carry out their operations. One important consideration within countries' HR systems is cross-border differences in workforce competencies. Workforce competencies are the knowledge, skills, abilities, and other talents that individuals in a given workforce possess. At a cross-national level, there is considerable variance among employees' competencies, especially with respect to their country-level literacy rates and educational attainment. Let's consider each of these in greater detail.

3.2.1   Literacy

A fundamental building block for advancement within all societies is literacy, or the ability to read. It is easy to imagine how, without this ability, employee competencies can be drastically limited within a given country. In countries with higher literacy rates, workforce competence is generally higher. As you can see in Figure 3.1, regions around the world differ greatly in the literacy rates of the potential workforce. For example, some countries in central Africa have a literacy rate of less than 50%, while other areas of the world such as the United States, Europe, and Australia have literacy rates over 95%.[2] With a workforce with a literacy rate under 50%, companies might be hard pressed to find suitable talent to perform many of even the most basic functions necessary for the success of their foreign subsidiaries. In contrast, as literacy goes up, the ability to find qualified individuals in host locations increases as well. It should not be surprising that many multinational locations are based in

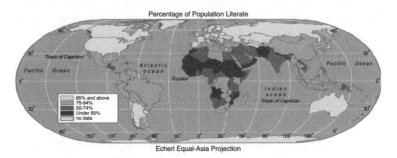

Figure 3.1   Literacy Rates Around the World

Source: Literacy Rates Across the Globe. Serbia & Montenegro Country Review 2006, p. 110; Abstract: The article presents a world map detailing literacy rates around the world (AN 23107546).

areas with higher levels of literacy such as North America, Europe, and Asia.

3.2.2 Educational Attainment

Closely related to literacy is the level and type of educational achievement. For example, one form of educational level is the level of tertiary attainment. Tertiary attainment refers to the proportion of a population that has achieved qualifications into advanced research programs and professional-level qualifications with high skill requirements, as well as individuals with occupationally oriented education that leads to access to jobs on the open labor market. On this dimension, Canada, Japan, and the United States outperform other countries such as Brazil, Italy, and Turkey. This does not mean the former countries' workforces are better in these different regions; rather, it means that the qualities of the workforce, particularly with regard to training for higher-level occupations and professions, differ in the ability of their populations to work in higher-level occupations.[3] If a multinational organization is looking to establish an operation or build partnerships around the world for higher-level positions, Canada and Japan might be more desirable than Brazil and Turkey to meet that need.

Closely related to tertiary education is a different indicator of educational achievement across countries provided by the Program for International Student Assessment (PISA). The PISA provides an assessment of the knowledge and skills of 15-year-old students in science, mathematics, and reading. Rather than looking at what achievements people in the workplace have already attained, PISA provides an indicator of the potential talents of the workforce now and into the future. As a result, this test is a good indicator of how well countries provide young, future workers with the key foundation elements necessary for life and learning after schooling.[4]

In 2006, over 400 000 students in 57 countries were assessed; the PISA results indicate some interesting differences across countries. With regard to scores on the science scale, Finland, Canada, and Japan were the top three while Mexico, Indonesia, and Brazil received the lowest marks. For the reading scale, the top three were Korea, Finland, and Canada. The bottom three countries were Brazil, Indonesia, and Mexico. In the top three for the mathematics scale were Finland, Korea, and the Netherlands and the bottom three were Brazil, Indonesia, and Mexico. While this is not entirely surprising, countries that performed well in one category tended to perform well in all three categories. The most logical explanation for this is that the educational systems in these countries provide a stronger foundation for all topics. From an HR perspective, an important interpretation of these data is that in Finland and Korea, entry-level workers will have higher levels of abilities received through their educational training compared to entry-level workers in Brazil or Mexico, whose country averages were much lower.

A more basic consideration for education level is the highest level of education attained by individuals in a country. Figure 3.2

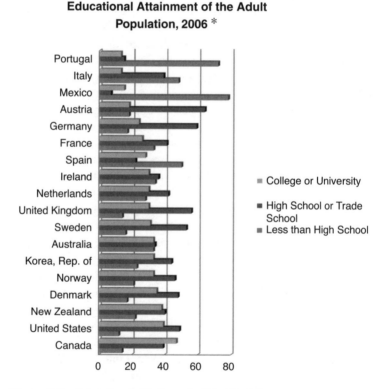

Educational Attainment of the Adult Population, 2006 *

Figure 3.2   Educational Attainment of the Workforce

Source: U.S. Department of Labor. March 2009. A Chartbook of International Labor Comparisons http://www.bls.gov/fls/chartbook2009.pdf.

represents data from the Organization for Economic Cooperation and Development (OECD) provided by the Bureau of Labor Statistics on the highest level of education attained by the adult population in a variety of countries.[5] As the table shows, in some countries, such as Canada, a high percentage of the workforce has a college or university education. This is compared to Portugal, Italy, and Mexico with a much smaller percentage of the workforce having a high-level education. In fact, in Portugal and Mexico, a good percentage of the population has less than a high school education. In contrast, in the United Kingdom, the United States, and Canada, more than 80 % of the adult population has at least completed high school.

3.2.3   Government Investments

An additional factor that influences the competencies of workers within a country relates to the extent of government investment in the workforce beyond education. For example, countries vary dramatically in the extent to which the government explicitly funds activities to enhance workforce competencies. One area that is particularly important with regard to workforce competencies is expenditure on research and development activities. For example, Sweden, Finland, Japan, and Korea lead OECD countries with a high level of gross domestic expenditure on research and development with expenditures exceeding 3 % of GDP. In contrast, Mexico and the Slovak Republic spend less than 0.5 % of gross domestic expenditure on research and development. The average level of investment for all OECD countries was 2.3 %.[6]

Closely related is an indicator regarding the differences in countries' governmental investment in knowledge creation. This indicator includes expenditure on R&D but also includes total expenditures on total higher education (public and private) and on software. According to this metric, the top three countries investing in knowledge acquisition are the United States at 6.6 % of gross domestic product, Sweden at 6.4 % of gross domestic product, and Finland at 5.9 % of gross domestic product. The lowest three countries with available data are Portugal, Greece, and Ireland.[7]

While these data capture a snapshot in time, 10 years earlier Sweden was also the highest spender on research and development while Mexico had the lowest expenditures. The trends of investment seem to be relatively stable over time and reflect the idea that in some countries, public policy and government priorities are more strongly focused on increasing the intellectual capital of the workforce. In other countries, the priorities simply are at a lower level of investment for developing various workforce competencies. Taken together, we can see how different regions of the world are more or less attractive as locations for foreign subsidiaries, as investments in offshoring locations, and as target areas for acquiring needed employees, all due to factors associated with literacy, education, and government investments.

3.3 Cross-Border Differences in Labor Economics

The previous discussion outlined important cross-border differences in the workforce competencies that exist around the globe. A second factor that is critical for managing HR issues in a multinational context relates to labor economics. Labor economics within a given country will affect the supply of available competencies, the ability to staff a given subsidiary, and workforce planning. Three labor economic issues are particularly relevant for managing talent across countries: unemployment rates, labor supply, and demographic trends.

3.3.1 Unemployment Rates

One of the most objective cross-border factors influencing HR in transnational contexts is the unemployment rate. According to the International Labour Organization (ILO), 61 % of the global population of working age (roughly 3 billion people) was employed in 2007 and the number of unemployed people was 189.9 million people. By region, the Middle East and North Africa had the highest unemployment rates (11.9 % and 10.8 %), followed by Latin America and the Caribbean, Central and Southeastern Europe (non EU), and the Commonwealth of Independent States (CIS) at 8.5 %. East Asia and South Asia had the lowest unemployment at less than 6 %.[8]

In 2008, these rates shifted, reflecting unequal patterns around the globe. For example, from 2007 to 2008 unemployment dropped to

10.3 % in North Africa and 9.4 % in the Middle East; it also dropped in Latin America to 7.3 %. However, as with 2007, the lowest 2008 unemployment rate was in East Asia (3.8 %), followed by South Asia (5.4 %) and Southeast Asia and the Pacific (5.7 %). The report shows that the three Asian regions – South Asia, Southeast Asia and the Pacific, and East Asia – accounted for 57 % of global employment creation in 2008. In contrast, the largest increase in a regional unemployment rate was observed in the Developed Economies and European Union region, from 5.7 to 6.4 %; the number of unemployed individuals in the region jumped by 3.5 million in one year, reaching 32.3 million in 2008.[9] In 2009, most countries' economies took a turn for the worse. For example, in May 2009, the US unemployment rate surpassed 9.0 % – a dramatic increase from roughly 5.0 % just one year earlier.

A country's unemployment level influences the availability of skills and workers. Higher levels of unemployment create a larger supply of workers with certain skills. In contrast, lower levels of unemployment force companies to work much harder to identify and hire qualified employees. Low unemployment is also often associated with the need for firms to pay increasingly higher wages to attract scarce talent. Relatively high unemployment (combined with high competence) in countries such as India and Ireland make them attractive locations for companies looking to expand internationally because they provide a relatively high number of skilled, available workers.

3.3.2   *Labor Supply*

Closely related to unemployment rates is the nature of a region's labor supply. While this is certainly influenced by unemployment rates (higher unemployment means greater supply), it is influenced by other factors as well. Two particularly important factors affecting the labor supply are the size of the labor force and the availability of specific skill sets.

Regarding the size of the labor force, among the OECD countries, the United States has the largest workforce, with 153.1 million workers in the labor force in 2007. In comparison, a combination of 15 European countries (Austria, Belgium, Denmark, Finland, France, Germany, Greece, Ireland, Italy, Luxembourg, the Netherlands,

Portugal, Spain, Sweden, and the United Kingdom) had 186.3 million individuals in the labor force. The US labor force is clearly the largest in this sample. At first glance, this would suggest that the US labor market is the most viable source for labor. However, this is a somewhat misleading indicator. The US makes up roughly 5% of the world's population. In comparison, China and India make up 20% and 17% respectively – over one third of the world's population.[10] Aside from the sheer size of the consumer market in these two countries, their labor force is vast. Even if China and India have lower literacy rates and/or educational attainment than the US and the EU, the number of people in those countries that have similar skills sets might exceed those within the US and the EU. Moreover, for entry-level jobs that require lower skill sets, China and India offer a tremendous opportunity for labor supply for multinationals around the world.

Population numbers alone can be misleading as an indicator of available talent, given that countries vary with respect to the percentage of women in the workforce (as a percentage of the entire workforce) and the percentage of women in managerial positions (as a percentage of all managers in a given country). A study by the OECD ranks countries based on the percentage of women with children who were employed in 2006. Countries in Europe have the greatest percentage of women in the workforce. For example, female employment rates are over 80% in Iceland and more than 70% in the Scandinavian countries and Switzerland. It is easy to see that the percentage of women in the workforce can greatly affect the size of the prospective labor pool.

In addition to size, an important consideration is a more basic assessment of the potential availability of qualified labor in specific occupations. Countries differ in the types of skills that their workforces have, as well as the level or supply of workers with those skills. For example, during the late 1990s, many of the dot.com companies faced a severe labor shortage of people in the United States with the appropriate computer skills. This was not a function of unemployment, but rather a function of the sudden demand for specific skills in the area of informational technology and computer programming leading up to the Y2K problem. In another demand-based example, there has been a growing trend to outsource programming, customer service, telemarketing, and similar work to India, particularly from the United States. As a result of the newly created demand, India has experienced labor shortages for other categories of professionals such as project managers, manufacturing, retail managers, sales clerks, and pilots in certain regions.[11]

Across countries in the OECD, the number of individuals who are entering fields of research has increased. The increases in research-oriented professionals, however, have not been equal across countries. Finland has over 15 researchers for every 1000 people employed, while India has less than one researcher per every 1000 people employed. For comparison purposes, the UK has 5.9 per 1000 people employed and the US has 9.6.[12] Taken together, these data suggest that India may be an ideal location for a firm's call center but may fall short on talent supply for a research center.

Knowing that firms are attracted to high labor-supply countries, workers are also increasingly aware and taking advantage of these employment opportunities in different countries. Some individuals have sought out opportunities in countries experiencing high global demand for their labor, such as in India or China.[13] According to the National Association of Software and Service Companies, in 2005, roughly 30 000 workers in information technology and outsourcing companies in India were from other countries.[14] Companies such as Microsoft, Intel, and Cisco Systems Inc. are increasing their investments in their overseas operations, so it is not surprising that individuals are continually relocating to countries in which the best prospects for job growth exist.[15]

3.3.3 Long-Term Demographic Trends

Taking an even longer term perspective, we can think about population growth rates across countries and how they may affect firms' long-term labor supply. For example, the three-year average annual growth rate was 2.34% for Ireland and 2.32% for Iceland. Worldwide, the average growth rate was 1.19%. In Hungary, Germany, and Poland, the growth rate was negative.[16] This means that some populations are increasing in size while others are shrinking. If these trends continue (and they tend to be fairly stable), this suggests that Ireland and Iceland would have a greater supply in the future than Poland, Hungary, and Germany if everything else is held equal. Consequently, it may make more sense to target Ireland or Iceland for future offshoring sites rather than Poland to avoid long-term labor shortages.

A different perspective on factors that may have an impact on labor supply and demand relates to the life expectancy of the population. Life expectancy in OECD countries reached 79 years in 2006. In some countries, such as Australia and Japan, life expectancy is above 80, while it is lower in other countries such as the Russian Federation (66.6 years) and Turkey (71.3 years).[17] Outside of OECD countries, however, there is considerably more variance in life expectancy. According to the World Health Organization, countries in the Africa region averaged a life expectancy of 52 years, with a child mortality rate of 145 per 1000 births. Compared to the life expectancy of the US (76 years) and child mortality rate of the US (19 per 1000 births), it is clear that life expectancy can vary greatly around the world.[18]

Another important long-term trend that affects labor supply relates to the aging of society. By the year 2050, Japan and Korea can expect over 38% of their workforce to be aged 65 or older. Throughout the world the average is 16.2% of a country's population to be in this age group. At the other extreme, some countries are very young, such as South Africa and Mexico.[19] The age distribution of a country's labor force affects multinationals in several ways. First, it clearly influences the size of the labor force not only today, but also in the future. In the United States and Japan, companies are struggling to identify how they will cope with an increasing drop in the size of the labor force that continues as the baby boomers retire. Another aspect is that the age distribution of the population influences consumer behavior. There are differences in spending patterns and demand for products and services at different stages of the life cycle. As the consumer market ages, this might affect demand for services and products of multinational companies differentially around the globe.

Given differences in the demographics and supply of global labor forces, companies are often forced to engage in different tactics for parts of their business in different global locations to respond to the unique labor force trends. As we will discuss in later chapters, where multinational companies recruit, their use of alternative forms of employment, and the amount of training they must provide will be influenced by the competencies of the workforce in locations in which they operate. Similarly, in some regions companies may be forced to pay high wages and provide excessive benefits to lure employees from competing firms due to low unemployment or a limited supply. In other regions with labor surpluses, these tactics are not likely to be necessary.

3.4 Cross-Border Differences in Employment Regulations

The third cross-border difference that we highlight relates to employment laws and regulatory differences. The challenge with comparing employment laws is that the differences are substantial and it is not possible to cover all permutations of these differences. In this chapter we highlight some broader differences that underscore the variance across countries on these issues.

3.4.1 Terms of Employment

One fundamental difference that exists across countries is the nature of their legislative oversight of terms of employment. As an example of how laws regulating terms of employment may differ across countries, let's consider the differences between Mexico and the United States. A comparison between Mexican and US labor laws reveals both similarities and differences between the two countries. Both countries' labor laws cover a wide range of employment-related issues. Mexican labor laws provide some protections that do not exist in the US. For example, Mexican Federal labor law requires written employment agreements and provides standards for just cause discharge for nonunion workers. At the same time, however, legal protections regarding wage rates are more favorable for US workers. Penalties for wage violations in Mexico are also quite low, thereby failing to encourage compliance with wage rates. This is a broader concern with labor laws in Mexico, i.e. there is not an effective infrastructure to enforce the laws, so violations may go unnoticed and laws unenforced.[20]

Compared to Europe, the US has considerably less legislative control over employment relationships. European countries, in contrast with the US, have greater regulations regarding recruitment and dismissals, for example, which exceed those regulations with which US companies must comply.[21] But it is not just in comparing the US to other countries that differences are found. For example, countries such as Portugal, Spain, and France have much more extensive employment laws than New Zealand, Japan, and Hong Kong with regard to legislation overseeing alternative employment contracts, working times, overtime, leaves, amount of notice and severance required, and dismissal procedures.[22]

In addition, countries differ in how much statutory protection exists regarding collective relations laws that influence labor union power over working conditions, the right to unionization, and collective bargaining. In an assessment of cross-border comparisons of countries on these dimensions, Canada, Malaysia, and the United Kingdom receive low scores while Peru, France, and Kazakhstan receive higher scores.[23] This particular finding suggests that workers in Canada have less protection regarding labor relations than workers in France or Peru.

We can also consider countries in terms of the protections they provide employees. In an interesting assessment, the Doing Business project (http://www.doingbusiness.org/) provides measures of business regulations and their enforcement across 181 economies. In one assessment they provide data on factors such as the difficulty of hiring, difficult of firing, and firing costs. Difficulty of firing is an index that captures how much notification and what approval requirements must be obtained to terminate a redundant worker, how much obligation exists to reassign or retrain these workers, and rules for reemployment. The costs of firing refer to how much notice is required, how much severance is required, and the penalties that might be assessed when terminating a redundant worker.[24] In Mauritius, for example, an employer is required to give three months' notice before a redundancy termination, and the severance pay for a worker with 20 years of service equals five months of wages. No penalty is levied. Altogether, the employer pays the equivalent of 35 weeks of salary to dismiss the worker.[25] Table 3.1 provides some data on these differences and a few other related metrics.

3.4.2   Benefits

There are also differences in legal and cultural mandates regarding employment benefits. Let's consider the issue of vacation time. In

Table 3.1 Doing Business: Statistics on Difficulty of Hiring and Firing Workers

Region or Economy	Difficulty of Hiring Index	Rigidity of Hours Index	Difficulty of Firing Index	Rigidity of Employment Index	Firing Costs (weeks of salary)
OECD	25.7	42.2	26.3	31.4	25.8
Australia	0	0	10	3	4
Brazil	78	60	0	46	37
Spain	78	60	30	56	56
Indonesia	61	0	60	40	108
Finland	44	60	40	48	26
Singapore	0	0	0	0	4
United States	0	0	0	0	0
Austria	0	60	40	33	2
China	11	20	50	27	91
Mauritius	0	20	50	23	35
Vietnam	11	20	40	24	87
Saudi Arabia	0	40	0	13	80
Germany	33	60	40	44	69
Mexico	33	40	70	48	52
Sweden	33	60	40	44	26
Czech Republic	33	40	10	28	22
Netherlands	17	40	70	42	17
Poland	11	60	40	37	13
Argentina	44	60	0	35	95
Dominican Republic	44	40	0	28	88

Source: The Doing Business project Employing Workers
http://www.doingbusiness.org/ExploreTopics/EmployingWorkers/?direction=
Asc&tsort=2

the United States, there is no legal mandate for vacation time. Some countries within Europe, in contrast, have requirements for paid time off from work. Even when negotiated, there are big differences in how much vacation time employees receive across countries. In the US, vacation time is typically associated with length of service. A common approach might be to start workers in the United States with 10 days' vacation and then provide an additional week of vacation at every five or more years of service. In contrast, many European Union countries have a statutory minimum of 20 days

Table 3.2   Government and Private Expenditures on Health Care

	Government Expenditures as % of total expenditures on health care in 2006	*Private expenditures as % of total expenditures on health care in 2006*
Argentina	45.5	54.5
Belgium	72.5	27.5
Canada	70.4	29.6
India	25.0	75.0
Italy	77.2	22.8
Malaysia	44.6	55.4
Netherlands	80.0	20.0
United Kingdom	87.3	12.7
United States	45.8	54.2
Vietnam	32.3	67.7

Source: World Health Organization. *World Health Statistics 2009, Table 7: Health expenditure.* http://www.who.int/whosis/whostat/EN_WHS09_Table7.pdf.

after one year of service, with an additional 10 public holidays.[26] In our discussion of Lincoln Electric, legally mandated differences in the allocation of vacation days and paid time off were one of the challenges that Lincoln dealt with when it entered into different international markets.

In addition to vacations, countries vary greatly in the coverage of health care expenses by the government versus from private expenditures. Table 3.2 provides a comparison of a sample of countries with regard to the amount of government expenditures as a percentage total of total expenditures on health care in 2006.[27]

Countries differ in their legislation and public policy toward health coverage, and these differences directly influence business decisions related to managing the workforce. A company operating in the United Kingdom or the Netherlands, for example, will experience lower health care costs than a company operating in a country that provides a much lower percentage of government support for health care. In contrast, health care expenses for multinational organizations will increase in countries such as the United States and Vietnam, where the burden of health care coverage does not rest predominantly on the government. As an example, it is reasonable to conclude that operating in a low coverage country will be associated with greater benefits-related costs than operating in countries offering higher coverage.

3.4.3   Regional Guidelines

In addition to legal mandates within countries, there are also agreements related to multinational organizations that go beyond the borders of any one country and cover multiple countries. One such set of agreed upon employment guidelines is the OECD Guidelines for Multinational Enterprises. The OECD is a forum of 30 countries that work together to address social, economic, and environmental challenges related to increasing globalization. The participating member countries are: Australia, Austria, Belgium, Canada, The Czech Republic, Denmark, Finland, France, Germany, Greece, Hungary, Iceland, Ireland, Italy, Japan, Korea, Luxembourg, Mexico, the Netherlands, New Zealand, Norway, Poland, Portugal, Slovak Republic, Spain, Sweden, Switzerland, Turkey, the United Kingdom, and the United States. Text Box 3.1 highlights these guidelines for the OECD. These countries have collaboratively developed influential guidelines and standards for multinational enterprises relating to a variety of issues such as employment and industrial relations, human rights, and taxation. The OECD Guidelines for Multinational Enterprises can be found online at: http://www.oecd.org/dataoecd/56/36/1922428.pdf.

Box 3.1   Organization for Economic Cooperation and Development (OECD) Guidelines

The *Guidelines* are recommendations addressed by governments to multinational enterprises operating in or from adhering countries (the 30 OECD member countries plus eleven non-member countries: Argentina, Brazil, Chile, Egypt, Estonia, Israel, Latvia, Lithuania, Peru, Romania and Slovenia). They provide voluntary principles and standards for responsible business conduct, in a variety of areas including employment and industrial relations, human rights, environment, information disclosure, competition, taxation, and science and technology.

Although many business codes of conduct are now publicly available, the *Guidelines* are the only multilaterally endorsed and comprehensive code that governments are committed to promoting. The *Guidelines'* recommendations express the shared values of governments of countries that are the source of most of the world's direct investment flows and home to most multinational enterprises. They aim to promote the positive contributions multinationals can make to economic, environmental and social progress.

The *Guidelines* have several distinguishing features that helped them gain acceptance and continue to ensure they are supported. First, observance of the *Guidelines* is voluntary. Their non-binding nature, however, does not imply less commitment by Adhering Governments to encourage their observance. The active system under which the *Guidelines* are promoted and implemented attests to the importance Adhering countries give the *Guidelines.*

Also, the *Guidelines'* basic approach is balanced. The assumption is not that enterprises need to be "controlled" but that internationally agreed guidelines can help prevent misunderstandings and build an atmosphere of mutual confidence and predictability between business, labour and governments. A continuing, pragmatic approach has characterised the *Guidelines* process and helped make them work.

Although they are addressed to enterprises, the *Guidelines* need the support of the business community, labour representatives and non-governmental organisations in order to be effective. The countries adhering to the *Guidelines* will work with all of these actors and there is every reason to believe that constructive collaboration will develop that helps the business community define and achieve appropriate standards of conduct. In addition, the post-Review period is likely to be one of expanding adherence to the Declaration of which the *Guidelines* is an integral part. Several non-OECD members have already adhered to the *Guidelines* and others that are willing and able to meet the disciplines in the Declaration would be welcome too.

Source:
Organisation for Economic Cooperation and Development website. The OECD Guidelines for Multinational Enterprises: Frequently Asked Questions. Accessed July 1, 2009.
http://www.oecd.org/document/58/0,3343,en_2649_34889_2349370_1_1_1_1,00.html.

According to the OECD 2009 annual report, the OECD is a member organization that

> ... provides a forum where governments can compare and exchange policy experiences, identify good practices and promote decisions and recommendations ... The Organization's mission is essentially to work for a stronger, cleaner, fairer world economy ... The organization places a high priority on deciphering emerging issues and identifying policies that work in order to help policy makers.[28]

The OECD is exemplary in that it is a voluntary agreement among various countries to share information and to strive to assist one another in solving common problems, identifying good practices, and coordinating international policies that benefit all countries involved. The group works with participating member states to achieve a variety of objectives, such as helping to shape policy that influences how business is done, where investments should be made, and how to help the environment. While not a legally enforcing entity like a national government, the OECD's prominence in oversight of international business means that its policies and recommendations carry considerable weight among countries on a variety of issues, many of which have an impact on how multinational organizations operate.

Related to this, the countries in the European Union also agree to subscribe to directives and the philosophy of EU labor laws. What is interesting about regulations in this region is that countries have their own distinct labor systems but also operate within a broader oversight of the EU labor system. For example, France and Germany have distinct legislative practices regarding employment and labor law. Yet both must operate within, and in compliance with, the guidelines of the EU. The EU has a variety of directives in place regarding issues related to diversity and discrimination, gender equality, mobility, rights at work, inclusion and equality, health and safety, and labor laws on issues such as working conditions, data protection, and privacy. For example:

- The EU directive on the protection of young people at work insists that member states must prohibit the employment of children (i.e. those under the age of 15 or still in compulsory education) with some notable exceptions related to cultural, artistic, sports, and advertising activities.

- The EU directive on Individual Employment Conditions states that every employee must be provided with a document containing information on the essential elements of his contract or employment relationship. The place of work must be specified, as must the initial basic pay and other remuneration. And there must be descriptions of the work, working times, leave entitlements, and the arrangements for either side to give notice.[29]

These two directives are representative of a broader array of directives that exist within the European Union and are managed by the European Commission's Directorate-General for Employment, Social Affairs and Equal Opportunities, who works towards the creation of more and better jobs, an inclusive society, and equal opportunities for all. As noted on the European Commission website,[30] some examples of key objectives are:

- More and better jobs through the European Employment Strategy (which brings national policies closer in this field) and the European Social Fund (€ 9 billion per year managed in partnership with the Member States).
- Free movement of workers and coordination of social security schemes, which means that every EU national has the right to work and to live in any EU country and that people who move between countries are not disadvantaged in relation to social security including health care.
- Better working conditions through common minimum standards in the workplace, by supporting and developing social dialogue at European level, by modernizing labor relations, and by assisting EU workers who want to be mobile.
- Social inclusion and non-discrimination by supporting efforts to combat poverty and social exclusion, reform social protection systems, assess new demographic and social developments, take action against discrimination, promote fundamental rights, and enhance the integration of disabled people.
- Equality between men and women through legislation, programs designed to improve equal opportunities for women and men, and ensuring that the gender issue is taken into account in all fields of Community action.

From a practical perspective, these directives serve as minimum requirements for member countries of the EU. The member states must then provide a similar or more rigorous standard to protect the rights of employees throughout. If a company is considering operations with the European Union, familiarity with these directives serves a vital role to ensure compliance with the legal issues. But it is important to remember that these directives are not the same as the specific laws within each country. Countries comply with these regulations but may do so in different ways and with more stringent standards. It is imperative to be intimately familiar with the legal system within the specific country where you are considering operating.

3.5 Cross-Border Differences in Employee Representation

The fourth cross-border difference that directly influences HR in global business relates to unions and labor relations. Two factors are very important in this regard: the presence and role of unions and the requirements for representation in different countries.

3.5.1 Unions

Around the world unions serve a vital role in representing the interests of union members and providing a collective voice to individual workers in negotiating for fair working conditions with organizations. While unions' influences around the world are considerable, unionization rates varies considerably from country to country. For example, in the US, union representation was just over 12 % of the workforce in 2008.[31] In contrast, union density in Mexico in recent decades has been about 20 %. However, it varies from 3 % for construction and commercial sector workers to up to 70 % for education workers (teachers at all levels of instruction).[32] The labor union participation rate in Korea dropped from 25 % in 1977 to 10 % in 2005. Other countries have also experienced declines in union density. The union density in Sweden, while still very high, dropped from 83 % to 79 % between 1995 and 2000. In Australia the drop was more significant, moving from 35 % to 25 % over the same time period.[33]

As these data show, on a global level there is a trend of decline in union density overall, but relative union representation around the world varies greatly.

In addition to the amount of representation, unions also vary in the role and influence they hold within their countries. For example, European countries are much more heavily unionized than many countries elsewhere in the world. What is also an important aspect about unionization in Europe is the role of government oversight and involvement in union representation. Many countries in Europe are supportive of union representation and other forms of collective representation such as work councils and participation.[34] Another example is the All China Federation of Trade Unions (ACFTU), the largest union in China. In October of 2008 the AFCTU blacklisted several multinational corporations such as Dell, Wal-Mart, Eastman Kodak, McDonald's, KFC, and Samsung Group. In November of the same year, Wal-Mart made an announcement that workers in China could set up trade unions. While the AFCTU is not viewed as a powerful union in China, given its alliances with political leaders it provides a means to influence labor peace in China.[35] The ACFTU provides an interesting contrast in union activities which tends to be independent from government activity, since the ACFTU is a product of the Chinese Communist Party and the involvement of the state in its union activities is notable. As a result, serving the union may have come secondary to serving the party and country. Recently, however, new legislation was passed that went into effect in 2009 entitled Law of the People's Republic of China on Employment Contracts. This law, which provided additional influence to unions and allowed workers to have labor contracts, has led to an increase in wages.[36]

3.5.2   *Representation and Works Councils*

A specific form of representation that has garnered considerable attention is the works councils most famously deployed in Germany. In Germany, works councils have a legal right to co-determine employment-related issues such as annual leave and disciplinary policies and procedures. The law provides works councils with the right to veto in employment-related issues. Because of this, managers must work collaboratively with works councils before introducing any changes or else risk veto of their proposals.[37]

Works councils maintain information, consultation, and co-determination rights. Managers must provide the works council with timely and comprehensive information to enable it to carry out its function. This information may refer to new working methods or a reduction in operations. Consultation rights cover structural alterations to the facilities (plant and equipment), working methods that impact how jobs are performed, and manpower planning, including dismissals.[38] German works councils do differ from other European counterparts in their codetermination on matters related to the commencement and termination of working hours, overtime and reduced hours, leave arrangements, employee monitoring, fixing job and bonus rates, remuneration arrangements, health and safety issues, and other forms of performance-based pay.[39] Companies with more than 1000 employees allow works councils to help establish guidelines for the criteria used to transfer workers within the organization.

Other regions of the world may follow a pattern of representation similar to these legally mandated works councils. For example, there are larger groups of social enterprises that exert collective pressures and influences on organizations. One example is the European Works Council. European Works Councils (EWCs) are standing bodies providing for the information and consultation of employees in Community-scale undertakings and Community-scale groups of undertakings as required by the 1994 European Works Council Directive (Directive 94/45/EC).[40]

The primary aim of these EWCs is to enhance the rights of employees to information that might impact workers' interests. One of the important aspects of this is that the EWCs work to ensure that information from management related to employees in one participating state of an MNC which might impact employees in another participating state is communicated to all workers. To be covered under the directive, an enterprise must be a member state with at least 1000 employees in participating states and at least 150 employees in each of at least two member states. This means that companies in countries that are not directly under this directive from 1994, such as the United Kingdom, are bound by it in those of their divisions that are located in participating states and that meet the threshold number of employees.

According to the European Trade Union Institute EWC database, some 881 EWCs in 858 multinational companies were active in 2008, representing 15.6 million workers. These represent only a third of all companies concerned. This is due to the fact that the introduction of EWCs is not automatic but requires either the initiative of central management or "the written request of at least 100 employees or their representatives in at least two undertakings or establishments in at least two different Member States".[41]

EWCs vary somewhat across countries and companies. In some companies EWCs are mostly an employee-side committee, while in others they are really a joint employee–management committee. At Pirelli and Riva, management's interests are represented by a single member of management, while other companies such as Volkswagen and Bayer have much more involved managerial participation in the EWCs.[42] Typically, HR directors of the corporate management are involved with the EWCs.

Interestingly, countries vary in terms of the form of representation (union representation, works councils, and joint consultation committees) that is most prevalent. Union representation is the most typical across countries and can be seen in countries such as Japan, Italy, Australia, and the United States. Joint consultation, however, has seen growth in use. In joint consultation committees, there is not a formal role for unions but there is informal collaboration and cooperation between members of the union and management. The goal is to share information and raise concerns prior to formal negotiations or discussions.[43] The form of representation that is mandated in different regions is important, as it directly influences how subsidiary locations will be run; it also influences the requirements for worker representation in managerial decision making around the world.

3.6   Other Cross-Border Differences Affecting the Management of People

Although we will discuss cultural differences in much more depth in Chapter 4, it is important to touch briefly on cultural and comparative differences in how different countries approach the management of workers. The United States, for example, is known as one of the most individualistic and achievement-oriented countries. This perspective is clearly prevalent in the reliance on merit-based pay programs, individual incentive systems, and individual-oriented performance evaluations. Aside from these issues, however, there are also country-specific norms regarding the management of employees on issues such as hours worked and competitive wages.

3.6.1 Hours Worked

There is considerable variability in the average number of hours worked across countries. Korean workers lead the world in the average number of hours worked with 2305 hours per year in 2007. In the United States that average was 1794, in Australia the average was 1722, in France the average was 1561, and in the Netherlands the average was 1392 hours per year. This means that from a broader perspective, we can see that the average work week is lower in continental Europe (France, Germany, Sweden, Italy) and highest in Asian countries (Japan and Korea). The US and Canada are in the middle.[44] While this reflects cultural norms to a large degree, and legal mandates in some cases, it presents interesting challenges for managing multinational operations. For example, if a company from Korea wants to establish an international presence in the Netherlands, they will not be able to simply adopt their Korean approach to the work day, as the average worker in the Netherlands works only 60% as many hours as the average worker in Korea.[45] This might increase the number of staff that are needed to operate in the Netherlands to perform the same level of work as in Korea – providing an additional consideration in terms of efficiency of international jobs and structures.

3.6.2 Competitive Wage Rates

In addition to norms regarding hours worked, there are vast differences across countries regarding average wages. Figure 3.3 shows that the average wages in manufacturing jobs for countries such as Mexico, Brazil, Taiwan, and Hong Kong are less than 25% of those in higher wage countries such as Norway, Denmark, Switzerland, and Austria.

There are still significant pay rate differences around the world and even within countries. In a 2007 study by the Hay Group, the buying power of US managers was equal to $ 104 905 compared to Saudi Arabia and United Arab Emirates managers who were at the

**Average Compensation Costs for Production Workers in
Manufacturing in U.S. Dollars – 2006**

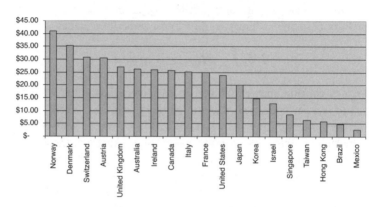

Figure 3.3 Average Compensation Costs for Production Workers in
Manufacturing in US Dollars – 2006

Source: U.S. Department of Labor, Bureau of Labor Statistics, *International Comparisons of Hourly Compensation Costs in Manufacturing, 2006,* http://www.bls.gov/news.release/ichcc.nr0.htm.

top of the list at $ 220 000. Managers in the emerging countries of
Russia, Turkey, and Mexico had average salaries of $ 150 000.[46] By
2010, all types of firms in Vietnam, where wages have traditionally
been extremely low, will be required to pay a common monthly
minimum wage to workers. The wage requirement is designed to
create equality and meet international economic integration.[47] In
March 2004, the Ministry of Labor and Social Security in China
issued minimum wage regulations for the first time.[48] In February
2008, the minimum monthly wage in Guangzhou, the capital city
of Guangdong province, was 860 Yuan or $ 120. Average minimum
wages in China have been growing in double digit percentages for
the past several years.[49] In the US, at $ 7.25 an hour, the minimum
monthly wage is $ 1257. Although the difference between these two
minimum monthly wages sounds quite significant, the minimum
wage in China might actually have equal or greater buying power
than the minimum wage in the US. As this discussion demonstrates,
there are significant differences in the specific practices that are used
in different countries, differences that are important to understand
as companies venture into different regions of the world in their
multinational business ventures.

3.7 Chapter Conclusions

Globalization magnifies the importance of the cross-border differences in workforce competencies, labor economics, employment law, and employee representation that are unique to each country. The average education level of the workforce, the occupational background, and the supply of workers with different skill sets establish the parameters for the amount of autonomy, discretion, and variety companies can feasibly build into different jobs. Companies must be attuned to the composition of the relevant labor force trends when assessing which approaches to managing employees are most likely to be successful in different scenarios. This is the essence of the view to "think globally and act locally". In doing so, it is important to acknowledge regional differences and adapt the management of people accordingly. There are several challenges that you should consider as you think about how to manage a workforce around the globe.

The availability of labor varies. When considering establishing operations in foreign countries, be aware that countries with low levels of skills (or facing a shortage of workers with certain skills) are less attractive locations for international operations, while countries with high levels of skilled workers are more attractive. For example, countries such as Mexico, Brazil, and Taiwan have a large supply of workers with desired skills who command relatively low wages compared to US companies. This is one reason why many companies have established *maquiladoras* (US-owned manufacturing plants located in Mexico); they provide labor for much lower costs than in the United States. Other countries are more attractive for companies that need a more highly skilled workforce. One reason that US companies increasingly offshore facets of their operations to India is the availability of relatively highly skilled workers who command lower labor costs.

How you manage must vary. While the essence of thinking globally and acting locally is to recognize that there are differences in preferences, tastes, norms, and cultures in different regions of the world, it is important to recognize that there are more structural and institutional factors that influence how you manage employees. In some countries, there are regulations on pay rates, bonus rates, benefits, and other forms of remuneration that do not exist in other countries. It is important to be aware of those factors, their potential costs and benefits, and their impact on your ability to function effectively in a location. There are also patterns of employee representation that influence HRM. Some countries and regions have much greater unionization or legal rights to representation. The requirements to meet this may influence the options that you may choose from in how you manage your workers.

Consider coordination and delegation of HRM. If countries differ significantly, it is important to have a thorough assessment of the benefits and costs associated with consolidating HR activities within a parent organization or delegating to country locations. There are strategic reasons for these decisions, but the cross-border differences might justify one or the other. If you are operating in two or more countries that are quite similar in their labor supply, workforce competencies, employment rights, and employee representation, a single HR approach across countries might be effective. As the differences on these dimensions increase across your operational locations, the effectiveness of delegating to locations might increase. Recognizing the nature of the work environment in the countries in which you operate may help you avoid mistakes in the management of your talent around the world.

Notes

1   Begin, J. (1992). Comparative human resource management (HRM): a systems perspective. *International Journal of Human Resource Management* 3: 379–408.

2   "Literacy Rates Across the Globe" in *Serbia & Montenegro Country Review 2006*, p. 110; Abstract: The article presents a world map detailing literacy rates around the world; (AN 23107546).

3   Tertiary Attainment, *OECD Factbook 2009*, pp. 280–281. Accessed June 30, 2009 at http://lysander. sourceoecd.org/vl=1257422/cl=13/ nw=1/rpsv/factbook2009/09/01/03/ index.htm.

4   International Student Assessment, *OECD Factbook 2009*, pp. 196–199.

Accessed June 30, 2009 at http:// lysander.sourceoecd.org/pdf/factbook 2009/302009011e-09-01-01.pdf.

5   US Department of Labor. March 2009. A Chartbook of International Labor Comparisons, http://www.bls. gov/fls/chartbook2009.pdf.

6   "Expenditure on R&D" in *OECD Factbook 2009*, pp. 164–165. Accessed June 30, 2009 at http://lysander.sourceoecd.org/pdf/ factbook 2009/302009011e-07-01- 01.pdf.

7   "Investments in Knowledge" in *OECD Factbook 2009*, pp. 166–167. Accessed June 30, 2009 at http:// oberon.sourceoecd.org/pdf/ factbook 2009/302009011e-07-01- 02.pdf.

8 International Labour Organization. Press Release. ILO projects global economic turbulence could generate five million more unemployed in 2008. Accessed February 10, 2008 at http://www.ilo.org/global/About_the_ILO/Media_and_public_information/Press_releases/lang-en/WCMS_090085/index.htm.

9 International Labour Organization. Press Release. Unemployment, working poor and vulnerable employment to increase dramatically due to global economic crisis. Accessed July 27, 2009 at http://www.ilo.org/global/About_ the_ILO/Media_and_public_information/Press_releases/lang-en/WCMS_101462/index.htm.

10 US Department of Labor, March 2009. *A Chartbook of International Comparisons*. Table 5.1 – World population density, 2007, http://www.bls.gov/fls/chartbook 2009.pdf.

11 Kripalani, M., November 7, 2005. India's skills crunch: As the economy booms, companies scramble to find trained workers. *Business Week*, pp. 54–55; Anonymous, November 7, 2005. The perils of unskilled labor. *Business Week*, p. 148.

12 Researchers, *OECD Factbook 2009* – pp. 168–169. Accessed June 30, 2009 at http://masetto.sourceoecd.org/pdf/factbook2009/302009011 e-07-01-03.pdf.

13 Patel, V., December 14, 2005. India, Inc. *Newsweek*. http://www.msnbc.msn.com/id/10455090/site/newsweek/.

14 Lakshman, N., January 16, 2006. Where the jobs are: Subcontinental drift. *Business Week*, pp. 42–43.

15 Patel, V., December 14, 2005. India, Inc. *Newsweek*. http://www.msnbc.msn.com/id/10455090/site/newsweek/.

16 Evolution of the Population, *OECD Factbook 2009*, pp. 12–15. Accessed June 30, 2009 at http://masetto.sourceoecd.org/pdf/factbook2009/3020090 11e-01-01-01.pdf.

17 Life Expectancies, *OECD Factbook 2009*, pp. 242–245. Accessed June 30, 2009 at http://masetto.sourceoecd.org/pdf/factbook2009/30200-9011e-11-01-01.pdf.

18 World Health Organization. *World Health Statistics 2009*, Table 1 – Mortality and burden of disease. Accessed July 27, 2009 at http://www.who.int/whosis/whostat/EN_WHS09_Table1.pdf.

19 Ageing Societies, *OECD Factbook 2009*, pp. 18–19. Accessed July 27, 2009 online from http://puck.sourceoecd.org/pdf/factbook 2009/3020090 11e-01-02-01.pdf.

20 Posthuman, R. A., Dworkin, J. B., Torres, V., and Bustillos, D. L. (2000) Labor and employment laws in Mexico and the US: An international comparison. *Labor Law Journal* 51(3): 95–111.

21 Pieper, R. (ed.), *Human Resource Management: An International Comparison* (Berlin: Walter de Gruyter, 1990).

22 Botero, J. Djankov, S., Porta, R., and Lopez-De-Silanes, F. C. (2004). The regulation of labor. *The Quarterly Journal of Economics* 119(4): 1339–1382.

23 Ibid.

24 For more information on the calculation of these statistics see the Doing Business website at http://www.doingbusiness.org/MethodologySurveys/EmployingWorkers.aspx

25 2007. Employing Workers. Doing Business: Measuring Business regulations. Accessed July 9, 2009 at http://www.doingbusiness.org/MethodologySurveys/EmployingWorkers.aspx.

26 2003. Vacation Advantage for European Workers. *Worklife*, vol. 14, 12–13.

27 World Health Organization. *World Health Statistics 2009, Table 7: Health expenditure.* Retrieved July 7, 2009 at http://www.who.int/whosis/whostat/EN_WHS09_Table7.pdf.

28 OECD *2009 Annual Report.* Accessed July 7, 2009 at http://www.oecd.org/dataoecd/38/39/43125523.pdf.

29 European Commission website. *Employment, Social Affairs and Equal Opportunities, Working Conditions.* Accessed July 24, 2009 at http://ec.europa.eu/social/main.jsp?catId=706&langId=en&intPageId=202.

30 European Commission website. *Employment, Social Affairs and Equal Opportunities, About Us.* Accessed July 24, 2009 at http://ec.europa.eu/social/main.jsp?langId=en&catId=656.

31 AFL-CIO. *Trends in Union Membership.* Accessed July 27, 2009 at http://www.aflcio.org/joinaunion/why/uniondifference/uniondiff11.cfm.

32 Fairress, D. and Levine, E. (2004). Declining union density in Mexico, 1984–2000. *Monthly Labor Review*, September, 10–17.

33 Bamber, G., Shaun, R., and Wailes, N. (2004). Globalization, employment relations and human resources indicators in ten developed market economies: international data sets. *International Journal of Human Resource Management* 15(8): 1481–1516.

34 Brewster, C. (2007). Comparative HRM: European views and perspectives. *International Journal of Human Resource Management* 18(5): 769–787.

35 Dexter, R., Brade, R., Bernstein, A., and Zellner, W. (2004). China: A worker's state helping the workers? *Business Week.* December 13, Issue 1912, p. 61.

36 Lepak, D. P. and Gowan, M., *Human Resource Management: Managing Employees for Competitive Advantage* (Upper Saddle River, NJ: Prentice Hall. December, 2008) p. 208.

37 Dictionary of Human Resource Management, 2001. Codetermination, p. 43.

38 Addison, J. T., Schnabel, C., and Wagner, J. (1997). On the determinants of mandatory works councils in Germany, *Industrial Relations* (36)4: 419–445.

39 Addison, J. T., Schnabel, C., and Wagner, J. (2001). Works councils in Germany: their effects on establishment performance. *Oxford Economic Papers* 53: 659–694.

40 Eurofound, European Works Councils. Accessed July 27, 2009 at http://www.eurofound.europa.eu/areas/industrialrelations/dictionary/definitions/europeanworks-councils.htm.

41 Eurofound, European Works Councils. Accessed July 27, 2009 at http://www.eurofound.europa.eu/areas/industrialrelations/dictionary/definitions/europeanworks-councils.htm.

42 Gilson, C., and Weiler, A. (2009). Transnational company industrial relations: The role of European works councils and the implications for international human resource management. *Journal of Industrial Relations* 50(5): 697–717.

43 Bamber, G., Shaun, R., and Wailes, N. (2004). Globalization, employment relations and human resources indicators in ten developed market economies: international data sets. *International Journal of Human Resource Management* (15)8: 1481–1516.

44 Ibid.

45 US Department of Labor. March 2009. *A Chartbook of International Labor Comparisons.* http://www.bls.gov/fls/chartbook2009.pdf.

46 Anonymous. (2007). Managers in emerging economies winning on pay: Hay Group research finds US managers lose out on disposable income. HayGroup Press Release, July 16, 2007.

47 Anonymous. (2006). Vietnam: Common monthly minimum wage to be applied at enterprises by 2010. *Thai Press Reports.* July 21. Accessed at http://www.worldatwork.org/waw/globabl/global.jsp.

48 Anonymous. (2004). China sets minimum wage rules. *People's Daily.* Accessed October 22, 2006 at http://english.people.com.cn/200402/06/eng20040206_134134.shtml.

49 Zhou, M. (2008). China hikes minimum wages amid inflation. *SmartMoney* (February 28).

CHAPTER 4

Cross-cultural Differences

The Cultural Lens for Managing the Global Workforce

4.1 Sir Howard Stringer at Sony

When managing a global workforce it is critical to understand cultural differences in order to operate with cultural agility. *Cultural agility* is the ability to quickly, comfortably, and effectively work in different countries and with people from diverse cultures.[1] Cultural agility is a critical competence for those working in a multicultural or cross-national setting, especially for those in leadership roles. In 2005, a *New York Times* headline touted the importance of understanding cultural differences in business. It read: "Sir Howard Stringer's ascension to the top job at the Sony Corporation, making him the first non-Japanese executive to run the company, is the culmination of a career largely built on a special talent for making cross-cultural connections."[2] Howard Stringer is a native of Wales who graduated from Oxford and received a British knighthood in 1999. As a young documentary filmmaker living in the US in the 1960s, he found himself subject to the military draft and consequently served in Vietnam, earning a US Army Commendation Medal for meritorious achievement. (He became a US citizen in 1985.)

After returning from Vietnam in 1967, Stringer fulfilled one leadership role after another in the broadcasting and entertainment industry, first with CBS, where he became President of the News division and subsequently President of the corporation as a whole; and later with TELE-TV, a media and technology company formed by Bell Atlantic, NYNEX, and Pacific Telesis. He joined Sony Corporation of America in 1997 and was named CEO of the Tokyo-based Sony Corporation in 2005. In his new position, Stringer oversees a broadly multinational business that includes Sony Corporation of America, Sony Corporation's Entertainment Business Group, Sony BMG Music Entertainment (a 50-50 joint venture with the German company Bertelsmann AG), and Sony Ericsson (a 50-50 joint venture with the Swedish Telefonaktiebolaget LM Ericsson).

By all accounts, Stringer is highly regarded for his ability to work harmoniously with colleagues from multiple cultures – generational, national, and professional. Stringer's cultural agility[3] has served him well as he navigates the cultural intricacies of the Japanese business world while simultaneously leading the company's divisions in the US, Europe, and other countries around the world. In Sir Howard's words, "Adapting to cultural phenomena has actually become intrinsic to my personality . . . you either adapt or go under."[4] Howard Stringer clearly understands the importance of cultural differences and operates with cultural agility.

From the perspective of human resources, as an outgrowth of a country's cultural values, cultural differences will have an influence on the way in which human resources policies and practices are developed and implemented. For example, diversity management and stock options reflect the American cultural dimensions of receptivity to differences and individual orientation, respectively. Quality circles and open office space reflect the Japanese cultural dimensions of group orientation. Cultural challenges can be partially anticipated in multinational firms where human resources practices may be developed in one country and transferred to others.

4.2   What Is Culture?

Culture is to a society what memory is to an individual.[5] In his seminal work on culture, Dr Geert Hofstede defines culture as the "collective programming of the mind" which distinguishes the members of one group or category of people from another group. Culture results from common experiences of members of collectives and is transmitted across generations, providing the underlying norms which guide how people think, act, and behave. Culture is a learned phenomenon as people within any given nation share *socializing agents* such as a common history, legal system, art, literature, media, educational system, political system, economic system, and the like. These national-level socializing agents tend to produce similarities within nations in the form of *behavioral norms, attitudes,* and *values*. These national similarities are collectively considered to produce a nation's *culture*.

For a foreigner visiting a country for the first time, behavioral norms are the first aspect of culture he or she may experience because a culture's behavioral norms can be readily observed. You can sense and feel cultural differences through passive observation (experiencing the food, culture, shopping, etc.) and direct contact with host nationals (working on a team with nationals, leading, negotiating, etc.). These observable behaviors, norms, and customs are fairly easy to learn and imitate if needed. This easily acquired surface knowledge of the culture works adequately most of the time for purposes of experiencing a country as a tourist. You can learn much about the surface-level culture by simply taking a walk, eating lunch with coworkers, and going to the grocery store. While behavioral norms of culture are visible, many important aspects of culture, such as values and beliefs, are less visible and may take a long period of time to fully understand. See Text Box 4.1 for some typical observations one may experience when entering a different culture.

Box 4.1 OBSERVATIONS OF CULTURAL DIFFERENCES

When you experience an unfamiliar culture, try to...
- Observe prototypical leaders or experts (e.g. TV news experts, political leaders, business leaders).
- Observe formality of dress, speech, etc. and relationship orientation when in small retail stores, restaurants, etc.
- Observe communication and personal space on public transportation.
- Observe signs of formality and hierarchy (titles and greetings) in the office.

- Observe the number and accuracy of clocks in public spaces.
- Ask for recommendations for restaurants, shops, etc. – what is justifying the recommendation?
- Listen for the way people introduce themselves.
- Learn before you go – talk to colleagues, use online tools, read books, etc. in advance of business trips, meetings, and international assignments in foreign countries.

The metaphorical visualizations of culture have been compared to an iceberg, an onion, and an ocean. Symbolically, they each have a benign and somewhat deceptive visual surface with more power, interest, and challenge hidden underneath, belying what is on the visual surface. Figures 4.1 and 4.2 illustrate the surface culture compared to the deeper values and beliefs of a culture.

When you visit a foreign country, you cannot help noticing the surface – the prevailing style of dress, manner of communication, food preferences; layout of cities, homes, and offices. You quickly catch on to how people greet each other, the hours when restaurants and shops are open, how money is handled, and how to get directions to a destination. The inner or below-the-surface culture, however, is generally sensed over time as you learn the deeper values and attitudes prevalent among those in the culture. Because they lie beneath the surface, you will often encounter them without even knowing it. *Cultural attitudes* are shared preferences and often manifest themselves as unspoken opinions toward what is considered beautiful or ugly, respectful or rude, appropriate or inappropriate, risky or safe, desirable or undesirable, and the like. *Cultural values* are even more deeply embedded assumptions – fundamental principles taken for granted as widely accepted beliefs; sometimes cultural values cannot be readily articulated because they are assumed to be shared.

National-level cultural values may include acceptance of basic principles such as the right of independence, privilege of birthright, the mutability of nature, or the nature of virtues such as courage, honor, or integrity. National-level attitudes and values may or may not be readily visible, especially for those who have not spent a significant amount of time in a given foreign country, deeply experiencing the way of life, interacting with the nationals of that

Figure 4.1 The Visible Aspects of Culture
Source: From *Managing Across Cultures: The Seven Keys to Doing Business with a Global Mindset,* by Charlene Solomon and Michael Schell (McGraw-Hill, 2009).

country, etc. For the purpose of this chapter, national-level differences in behaviors, attitudes, and values are collectively referred to as *cultural differences.* In only these few pages we can begin to imagine how cultural differences may influence a wide array of HR practices, such as who should be selected and what makes them ideal candidates, what type of training should be delivered and by whom, how pay should be allocated and whether seniority or merit are relevant, what type of benefits are considered rewarding or desired, and the list goes on. As you read the remainder of the chapter, think about how various cultural differences will influence specific HR practices.

There are numerous books and articles written about work-related cultural differences, many stemming from the seminal work by Geert

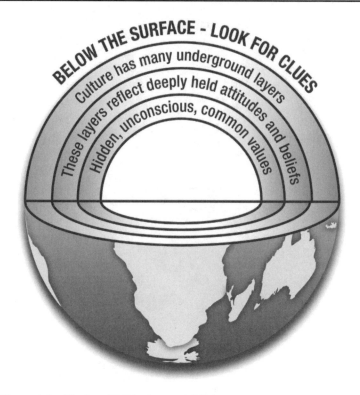

Figure 4.2 The Less Visible Aspects of Culture
Source: From Managing Across Cultures: The Seven Keys to Doing Business with a Global Mindset, by Charlene Solomon and Michael Schell (McGraw-Hill, 2009).

Hofstede on cross-national differences in work values.[6] Geert Hofstede's work originated at IBM in the late 1970s and uncovered that people in organizations – despite being members of a single company with a strong corporate culture – do differ in their work values cross-culturally. His finding is even more pronounced considering the fact that IBM in the 1970s and 1980s went out of its way to create the visible manifestations of cultural homogeneity. You may recall that IBM employees were famous worldwide for their professional uniform, consisting of a dark suit, white shirt, and conservative tie. In this context, where signs of culture were rarely visible, the underlying values of culture were still influencing relationships, communications, perceptions of time, and work behaviors. In fact, in a world that appears on the surface to be homogenizing across popular culture, manner of dress, and fast food, Geert Hofstede's findings are more relevant today than ever before, as the tangible signs that there may be underlying differences are disappearing in some contexts, while the actual differences are still present. Text Box 4.2 provides a brief summary of the cultural dimensions from Geert Hofstede's seminal research.

Box 4.2 HOFSTEDE'S CULTURAL DIMENSIONS

The seminal research conducted by Hofstede (1980)[7] examined 40 foreign subsidiaries of IBM to assess work-related values of people from many countries. Hofstede's seminal work is considered one of the most comprehensive studies of cross-cultural work-related values. The following is a brief description of his study and the general results.

Using a scale that had been translated into several languages, Hofstede collected data from IBM employees on their work-related values. The data were aggregated at the country level and factor analyzed. Based on the results of the factor analysis, work-related values were classified into four dimensions (1) power distance, (2) individualism versus collectivism, (3) uncertainty avoidance, and (4) masculinity versus femininity.

Power Distance
The first dimension is *power distance*, that is, the acceptance of unequal power among the levels of an organization. Mexico, Venezuela, Singapore, and Hong Kong, for example, will have more authoritarian (i.e. more accepted power distance) organizations, whereas, Austria, Israel, New Zealand, and Ireland tend to have organizations with more open relationships among the levels within their organizations. USA is less power distant.

Individualism versus Collectivism
The second dimension is *individualism/collectivism*. This is the degree to which group members' actions are either independent or dependent on each other. "More collectivist societies call for greater emotional dependence of members on their organizations" (p.152). Countries which are notably more individualistic are USA, Australia, Great Britain, and Canada. Countries which tend to be more collectivist are Peru, Pakistan, Columbia, and Venezuela.

Uncertainty Avoidance

The third factor is *uncertainty avoidance*, or how much threat or anxiety is felt in ambiguous situations. People in high uncertainty avoidant countries will adhere to rules and stay committed to employers longer than those in low uncertainty avoidant countries. High uncertainty avoidant cultures include Japan, Belgium, Portugal, and Greece. Low uncertainty avoidant countries include Hong Kong, Sweden, Denmark, and Singapore.

Masculinity versus Femininity

The fourth and last factor is *masculinity/femininity*, specifically, how masculine the nation's values are. If a country adheres to more masculine work-related values, it tends to be more focused on assertiveness interests such as the completion of the task, earnings, and advancement. A more feminine set of values would be focused on nurturing interests such as relationships with managers and coworkers, and cooperation among members in a work group. The most masculine countries were Japan, Austria, Venezuela, and Italy, whereas the most feminine countries were Denmark, the Netherlands, Norway, and Sweden.

4.3   A Framework for Cultural Differences

Understanding what to do in a given cultural situation presupposes that one can identify and understand cultural differences. To learn the information necessary to function effectively in multiple cultures, it helps to gather information and gain knowledge about cultural differences. The United States' State Department recognizes 194 independent countries around the world. Learning the subtleties of each of these countries' cultures, as you can imagine, would be a daunting task. Rather than memorizing endless lists of dos and don'ts, culturally agile professionals are able to learn and store collected bits of cultural knowledge into a *cultural framework* and apply the framework to a new (and unfamiliar) culture. They can gather these bits of cultural knowledge passively from books, magazines, newspapers, art, and from experiences.

It helps to have a cultural framework to organize the pieces of knowledge you gain. There are many cultural frameworks from the area of cultural anthropology.[8] For the purpose of managing the global workforce, three themes of cultural differences which reoccur across these frameworks are:

1   Gaining credibility
2   Communicating effectively
3   Working together successfully.

Each of these themes will be discussed in greater detail in the next section of this chapter. While all possible combinations of cultural dimensions and HR practices are beyond the scope of this chapter, it is important for you to consider the various ways culture may affect how to manage within a given cultural context and the challenges that might be present when introducing any given HR practice. Examples of the way cross-cultural differences may affect HR are provided in this chapter and also in Chapters 6 and 7.

4.3.1   Gaining Credibility

Credibility is perhaps the first step when a manager, team member, or associate from one culture enters into a company, work group, or subsidiary from another culture. One's credibility affects whether a manager's direction is followed, whether a team member's ideas are considered as plausible, whether a job candidate is deemed acceptable, and the like. Cross-cultural differences in credibility will influence HR practices in a variety of ways including who is selected for a job, promoted, given a leadership role, and any other HR practice involving the assessment of one person by others through a different cultural lens. It is most important to understand that cultures will vary on how credibility is gained (or lost) and, over time, how trust is gained (and lost). Cultures vary tremendously on the following factors influencing one's credibility. They are:

∎   Who you are and where you are from
∎   Who you know or what you know
∎   How you rank.

Who you are and where you are from. You can readily observe how well you fit into any given culture's conception of a professional. When you enter into a new culture, notice for example, the diversity of those in charge such as politicians, business leaders, and experts on television news programs. If you observe some diversity in gender and age, it is likely that your credibility (positively or negatively) will be influenced by those factors. In the Middle East, for example, you may notice that those in prominent and visible positions are predominantly male. In Italy, you may notice that they are attractive and more fashionably dressed. It is helpful to understand how your credibility and trust will be influenced by demographic and external factors, such as your high status, your academic degree, or your amazing Valentino suit.

Try to learn something about the universities from which politicians, business leaders, and other perceived experts have graduated. Is there much similarity? If so, the culture is likely a testing-based educational culture, one where the best students (regardless of family income) attend the best universities, such as in India, France, and Japan. (If you have an Ivy League degree, these are good countries in which to mention that personal tidbit of information.) The USA, in contrast, may place relatively less emphasis on one's educational institution for assessing credibility. While diversity and education may be somewhat easy to observe, it is more difficult to casually observe the cultures where your credibility can be eased by sharing your high-level birthright (or caste, as it is often called in Southeast Asia) – or reduced if you happen to come from a working class background. UNICEF, a division of the United Nations, estimates that caste can negatively affect 250 million people worldwide, many from countries in Africa and Asia. Colleagues from different cultures may differentially perceive your personal life story and you need to understand what it will do to your credibility. Sharing your working class roots may be viewed positively in some cultures such as in the USA and Australia, and may be viewed negatively in other cultures, such as India.

Who you know or what you know. Establishing credibility and building trust in some cultures can hinge on how you are introduced, who knows you, who respects you, who you are aligned with personally, and your own ability to form deep personal associations. These are relationship-oriented cultures. These cultures include many of the Latin European, Latin American, South American, and African cultures. In these cultures you will either need to be introduced by the right person or devote considerable time to developing the relationship before transacting business. You may observe family members or family friends working together more often in these "who you know" cultures because they are considered the people who will work hardest for you as vendor, coworker, subordinate, or other role.

Establishing credibility and gaining trust, in other cultures, is a function of your expertise, your client list, your achievements, what you know, and how you prove what you know. These are transactional cultures. In these cultures, including the USA, Germany, Canada, Australia, Switzerland, and many of the Scandinavian cultures, one can gain trust and credibility based on tangible demonstrations of qualifications and expertise. Unfortunately, credibility and trust can also be lost very quickly by a single incident of poor performance or a missed deadline because reputation is often built independently, without the credibility-bolstering influence of those with whom you are associated. These "what you know" cultures value highly objective assessment and believe that objectivity and professionalism may be compromised when one works with friends and relatives. Working with family members (unless it is a family-owned business) is often met with suspicion.

How you rank. Steve Jobs, CEO of Apple, is known for his very casual attire – Levis 501 jeans and a black turtleneck. His outfit, when worn in cultures where status and rank matter for ascribing professional credibility, is not exactly a credibility enhancer. Steve Jobs, because of his professional rank, will use fewer credibility points than most of us in the same outfit. The way individuals in a society react to power and authority is a distinguishing aspect of culture, providing insight as to the importance of your organizational level, job title, etc. In cultures where rank is not as important for credibility, you may observe people called by their first names (regardless of title, education, or level in the organization), business cards without job titles, and more personal interactions between supervisors and subordinates. Decision making is likely to involve input from workers in all levels of the organization.

In cultures where rank and status will matter when interpreting credibility, you may observe leaders with visible status symbols (nice car, larger office), more formality in dress (couture is critical in the executive suite) and titles, executive perquisites (e.g. dining rooms, parking spaces, use of limousines). Higher-level individuals are given greater respect in status-oriented cultures. Given that their rank gives them credibility in these cultures, they are expected to have expertise, be the decision makers, and provide direction. A high status individual can lose credibility in cultures such as India and Greece by asking a lower status individual for a suggestion, as the high status individual would be viewed as weak or ineffective. The same activity in a low status-oriented culture, such as Sweden or Canada, would likely raise credibility because these cultures tend to have equality as an ideal. In more hierarchical cultures, the expectations for each person are different according to his or her status. Other ways to lose credibility in high status cultures involve operating at a lower level than your status or rank ascribes. For example, wearing jeans to work, driving an old car, or having unrefined tastes would all serve to lower your credibility in status-oriented cultures such as Italy and France. Text Box 4.3 presents a checklist for understanding how you may gain credibility in different cultures.

Box 4.3 CHECKLIST FOR UNDERSTANDING THE DIFFERENCES IN THE WAY YOU CAN GAIN CREDIBILITY ACROSS CULTURES

1 How important is age and gender in this culture? How will I be perceived given my age and gender?
2 How important is educational attainment and the name of the university where I graduated? How will my educational background be perceived?
3 How important is my background or birthright? How will my own life story be perceived? Do I know what piece of it I should disclose openly?
4 How important are personal contacts and formal introductions in this culture? How will I be introduced – and by whom?
5 How important is building relationships before business is transacted? What will I do to build the relationship?
6 How important is organizational rank? How will my own rank be perceived?
7 How important are visible signs of status, such as dress and appearance? How will my appearance be perceived?

4.3.2   Communicating Effectively

As with credibility, communicating effectively across cultures will influence a myriad of issues such as communication issues among managers of different nationalities, within multicultural teams, and across work groups with multicultural representation. Communication issues will influence HR practices affecting how interviews are conducted, how training is delivered, how feedback is offered, and any other HR practice involving a sender and receiver of information (i.e. communications). Cultures vary on styles of communication and meaning that is ascribed to words and gestures. Specifically, cultures vary on:

- What your words will mean – compared to what you believe you are saying
- How you speak – and how your speech is interpreted.

What your words will mean – compared to what you believe you are saying. The American anthropologist Edward T. Hall found that in cultures where communication is indirect, or high context, it is difficult to understand the meaning of what was said unless you understand the contextual and cultural nuances around which the words were spoken (e.g. tone of voice, facial expressions, body language).[9] High context communications are most comfortable among those who can readily interpret what is not said, those who have common experiences and a similar lens for interpretation. If you have siblings, for example, there is a good chance that you all can accurately interpret the meaning of your mother's slight eyebrow raise or your father's change in vocal cadence. This common understanding among you and your siblings is an example of the way high context speech works. Those outside of your family would not derive the same meaning from your parents' subtle cues.

In high context communication cultures many things are left unsaid, letting the culture explain that which was fully intended. Communication in these high context cultures, such as Asia, the Middle East, Latin Europe, and Latin America, is subtle, nuanced, and may seem difficult to interpret to an outsider. Instead of saying "no," someone in a high context culture is likely to deny a request by saying, "We'll try" or "We'll see." In cultures with a direct or low context communication style, as in the Anglo, Germanic, or

Scandinavian cultures, whatever is said is meant, with little need for interpretation. In these cultures, you will observe more direct feedback being given and shorter written communications (e.g. email and instant messages). This cultural difference between indirect and direct communicators can be one of the more challenging in international management. People from high context communication cultures would be interpreting the entire context in which a communiqué is delivered, so when interacting with people from direct communication cultures, they are often told that they are "reading into things too much." On the other hand, individuals from direct communication cultures will read little meaning beyond the actual words spoken. Thus, in communicating with someone from a high context culture, they may have some difficulty understanding why one thing is said and something else is done.

How you speak – and how your speech is interpreted. Cultures differ in the extent to which they rely on formality to dictate the appropriate ways of behaving. In societies with greater formality, individuals will be called by their formal titles and will behave in the manner ascribed to that title; it is worth noting that dozens of languages around the world have a distinction between the formal and informal "you" (e.g. "*vous*" and "*tu*" in French), so that at least two levels of formality are built right into the language. In more informal cultures, it is often difficult to determine the status or position of people based on what they wear, how they interact, and the like. In formal cultures, you may observe people called by their title, little discussion of personal issues at work, formal greetings, and greater adherence to appropriate etiquette. In informal cultures, you will observe that people are called by their first names, dress more casually, and dine more informally.

In Mexico, for example, business is conducted in a far more formal way than what is typical in the US. Everyone is expected to dress in proper business attire, and the highest ranking person enters the room first. People do not use first names, or call each other "*tu*," in business unless they know each other very well. A variety of titles are used – not just Señor and Señora for Mr and Ms, but also Don and Doña, which signify higher status and a greater degree of respect and are often used for elders. Don and Doña are used with the person's first name, similar to the British "Sir Michael" or "Dame Joan" usage. For example, if Señor Pérez's given name is Miguel, he would be called Don Miguel as a sign of respect. In addition, it is important to use professional titles, including Doctor or Doctora; Licenciado/a (Lic.), which refers to anyone with a law degree or Bachelor's Degree; Contador Público (C.P.); Ingeniero (Ing.) to indicate an engineering degree; Arquitecto/a (Arq.); and Diputado/a (Dip.), which refers to a publicly elected official. In formal cultures, it is a significant faux pas to omit someone's title, not only in correspondence but also in everyday conversation. Formality is very easy to ascertain if you listen to how people are called.

Another highly visible communication difference is whether a culture is expressive and emotional or unemotional. The airport is about as far as one needs to go to experience this difference. In an expressive culture, the volume of speech will be louder, there will be obvious hand gestures, and there will be more tactile interactions (e.g. kissing on either cheek, walking arm in arm, public displays of affection). In the more unemotional cultures such as Finland and Japan, speech is restrained, far quieter, gestures are subtle and non-verbal cues, overall, are much more difficult to detect.

4.3.3 Working Together Successfully

There are many HR practices designed to help employees located around the world work together more effectively, such as programs to encourage shared values, tools to facilitate the sharing of documents or other forms of information, training programs for project teams, and the like. What is often overlooked is that these HR systems or practices designed to help people work together need to be understood in the context of the cross-cultural difference in the importance and value of work. Cultures vary on:

■ The importance of work
■ The importance and treatment of time
■ The comfort level with responsibility
■ The definition of "working together".

The importance of work. People vary across cultures in terms of the extent to which they value work. Some cultures value work in that they "live to work". These cultures believe that career success in its own right is valuable and will expend much effort to achieve it, even at the expense of a personal life. In these cultures, people will opt to work on weekends, take fewer and shorter vacations, and spend evenings answering emails and making work-related calls from home. A survey by Expedia.com found that over one-third of (already vacation-starved) Americans, who are known for placing great importance on work, will not take all of the annual vacation days to which they are entitled. Although people may complain that they are "never off duty," there is often an underlying pride in the effort and dedication they are applying to achieve career goals. In fact, a recent Harris Interactive survey indicated that "about one-third of employed U.S. adults (31 %) usually do not take all of the vacation days they receive each year".[10]

In contrast, people in balance-motivated societies such as northern Europe and South America believe that different spheres of one's life may coexist, but should not interfere with each other. Consider this portion of a Sweden-based IKEA's press release to announce a new store opening in the USA. In part, it said

> ... Drawing from the company's Swedish heritage, IKEA is committed to a flexible workplace that emphasizes a work/life balance and provides professional opportunities to people from all life situations. If an IKEA coworker needs to take time off to find a nursing home for an aging parent, be home to kiss their child before bed or have flexible scheduling to best juggle caring for a newborn, one can do so without worrying about risking their career aspirations.[11]

This is clear evidence of an organizational culture (calling on their national culture) that believes in working to live, rather than living to work. While professional careers may be very important, individuals tend to be motivated by the intrinsic rewards of the career rather than by promotions and pay raises. Public policy in balance-oriented cultures tends to mandate vacations ranging from 5 to 7 weeks per year, in addition to more numerous paid holidays (e.g. Ascension Day, August Bank Holiday, Boxing Day) and more family friendly parental leave policies. Taking this distinction into consideration, it is easy to see why Americans, who receive an average of only 14 vacation days per year, are often stereotyped as being "always in a hurry" by those in balance-oriented countries.

The importance and treatment of time. In cultures where time is controlled, time is treated as a commodity: It can be bought, spent, and wasted. The "time is money" maxim, attributed to the

American statesman Benjamin Franklin, exemplifies this attitude; it is also prevalent in northern Europe and in China. In controlled time cultures, you will observe punctual public transportation, more people wearing (and looking at) watches, more clocks in public places, meetings with a fixed start and end time, and a greater use of agendas. In cultures where time is viewed to have more fluidity, such as the Middle East and South America, there is greater emphasis on people and on how work is accomplished, as opposed to meeting and keeping deadlines. In fluid time cultures, you will observe people arriving beyond a scheduled time for social events and meetings, public transportation that does not adhere to a schedule, social events and meetings with a start time – but no end time.

As Geert Hofstede and his colleagues uncovered in his original research, cultures also differ according to their long-term and short-term time orientation. When one examines a long-range plan for a traditional Japanese firm (more past and future-oriented) the scope can extend both decades in the future and back in time to a deep connection to the founding principles of the firm. In contrast, the examination of a long-range plan for an American firm (traditionally more present-oriented) will be very short in scope (perhaps a few years, or even a few quarters). While the international markets are forcing publicly traded global firms to think more in the present, the time orientation is still a relevant cultural difference to consider. For example, present-oriented cultures will be more likely to make a plan and revise it as the context changes. The planning stage for their cultures is less important because so much of the future is unknown. A future-oriented culture will spend more time in the planning stage, anticipating the future, and then maintaining a closer adherence to that plan. Past-oriented cultures tend to have a greater reliance on how things have traditionally been done and will not easily adapt to new methods and ways of doing things.

The comfort level with responsibility. Jay Chapman is the Head of Communications for the British-based (healthy and fresh) fast-food restaurant chain, Pret A Manger. She describes one key to Pret A Manger's success is the empowerment given to every employee, regardless of level. She says "each team member is empowered from their first day at work to make their own decisions . . . it's not uncommon to find that if you've been in to Pret for your lunch every day for a week, the guy behind the till will recognise you and decide to give you Friday for free. The manager keeps an eye on things, but overall the team members are empowered to make their own decisions."[12] This level of empowerment may sound welcome to those comfortable with individual-level responsibility, but interpretation of the word "empowerment" varies greatly across cultures.

In cultures where autonomy is appreciated, empowerment is interpreted to mean that someone is trusted to set priorities and make independent decisions, is free to provide independent thought; empowerment is a desired and valued quality. In other cultures, the word empowerment is interpreted to mean abandonment – leaving the subordinate to his or her own devices, failing to provide adequate leadership. The difference, while extreme, reflects the way cultures interpret the desired amount of independent decision making; whether it is desired or whether there is a preference for direction to be given by a person of authority. This dimension is often evidenced in the number of levels (some real, some perceived) that exist in any given organization. In those cultures where autonomy is preferred, flatter organizations will exist with greater decision making throughout the organization. In cultures where direction is preferred, more layers of management will exist – even within teams and work groups.

The definition of "working together." In the highly collectivist cultures of the Middle East and Asia, relationships are strongly based on groups, whereas in highly individualist cultures of the USA and the UK, the basic relationship is the one-on-one dyad. In cultures valuing the group's interest, being a member of a successful team, organization, or unit is highly rewarding. In societies valuing the individual's interests, people expect to be personally rewarded and recognized for their unique contributions. The value of a team – and what it means to be a part of it – will vary greatly depending on a society's orientation on this dimension. In individual-oriented cultures such as those of the United States and Western Europe, individuals are recognized for their achievements with plaques and ceremonies, people readily talk about their personal contributions and achievements, people will sit alone eating or reading in public places, and an important indicator of business success is a personal office with a door that can be closed. Relationships in individual-oriented cultures are typically one-on-one; it is not unusual for someone to have a great many friends who are all strangers to one another, or who have only met each other on a few occasions, such as when the mutual friend hosted a large party. In group-oriented cultures, which tend to be more prevalent in Scandinavia, Asia, Latin America, and Africa, you may observe team competitions at work, coworkers eating lunch together on a daily basis, greater use of public transportation, and open office or communal office space. Relationships are centered on groups – when you become a friend of one person, you become a friend of his entire family, his circle of friends, and their families too.

4.3.4 Cautions for Understanding Cultural Differences

There are a few cautions to keep in mind as you understand cultural differences in the context of managing the global workforce. First is a phenomenon known as the "tourist fallacy." The tourist fallacy occurs when professionals believe that several business trips to a given country have produced in them a deep understanding of a culture's attitudes and values. A parallel to this is the overconfidence that people sometimes display when they have progressed to the intermediate level in learning a new language. Having mastered proper pronunciation and the ability to form correct sentences, the person will ask a question of a native speaker – only to be baffled by a rapid and complex reply that far exceeds their understanding. But, unfortunately, in the case of the tourist fallacy, the overconfidence is much less obvious. Business travelers may believe they have become fluent in the foreign culture, when in fact they do not yet understand the cultural nuances or underlying values of the culture.

A second mistake is to allow understanding of cultural differences to result in stereotyping. It is important to recognize that a country is not a pigeonhole into which all of its citizens neatly fit. In addition to national-level socializing agents, many other socializing agents influence the formation of a person's behavioral norms, attitudes, and values. Subgroups with identifiable socializing agents produce subcultures. Subcultures may include smaller geographic regions, professional groups, firms, and the like. These many influences, in combination, produce intranational diversity, the individual differences and variation existing among the nationals of any given country. In your interactions with people, it is just as important to recognize individual differences as it is to understand the norms of the culture.

4.4   Understanding Cultural Agility

As we have just read, the cultural differences matter when operating in a multicultural or cross-national setting and will influence how we manage people in determining which behaviors are the most appropriate. Using cultural differences in professional settings is far more challenging than studying or observing cultural differences; it is far more nuanced. The idea of cultural agility was coined by Paula Caligiuri in an effort to better describe the various ways professionals need to operate across countries and in multicultural settings. Cultural agility is not cultural adaptation; however, there are times when adaptation is critical. Cultural agility does not mean we should pretend cultural differences are nonexistent; however, there are times when a higher order professional demand will supersede cultural expectations. Cultural agility is not merging multiple cultures to create a new set of behavioral norms – but there are times when cultural integration is most important.

In the next section, we will discuss Caligiuri's three cultural orientations which collectively influence cultural agility. Cultural orientations manifest when people are working in a multicultural context or with people from a different cultural group. There are three cultural orientations present in those who are culturally agile – cultural minimalism, cultural adaptation, and cultural integration. In the most culturally agile individuals, each of these orientations will be leveraged depending on the contextual situation in which they are operating.

4.4.1   *Culture Minimalism*

Cultural minimalism is an orientation people have to reduce the perceived influence of cultural differences – either in one's own behavior or in the behavior of others. Cultural minimalists are especially well-suited to uphold the values of the organization and often require their subordinates and coworkers to adhere to the company's way of doing things. This is effective when global leaders need, for example, to uphold a corporate code of conduct or the corporate culture. In the most positive sense, cultural minimalists see colleagues as company employees first and will judge them on the behaviors they exhibit (often disregarding where they are from).

Cultural minimalists sense value in not labeling people by their culture or ethnicity and believe themselves to be very fair, or "blind" to differences. Cultural minimalism is a highly functional cultural orientation in situations where there are important strategic reasons to override or play down cultural differences.

The downside of cultural minimalism (especially in the absence of the other cultural orientations) is potentially derailing for global business leaders because, in most global leadership activities, some level of cultural sensitivity (or, at minimum, acknowledgement) is needed. Operating from the cultural minimalist orientation will often result in misunderstanding and frustration in a cross-cultural context. Cultural minimalists can sometimes derail because they are ineffective at behaving in culturally appropriate ways when working with cross-national teams, in international negotiations, communications with foreign clients, and the like. Cultural minimalists are often easily frustrated with any discussion of global diversity, and they may feel inauthentic – as if they are "putting on" behaviors – when they behave according to unfamiliar customs.

4.4.2 Cultural Adaptation

Cultural adaptation is an orientation people may have to be sensitive and strive to adapt to the nuances of cultural differences, often leveraged in situations requiring professionals to behave in the most culturally appropriate ways to be successful. The cross-national sales scenario is a typical case where cultural adaption is helpful in order to be successful. In her research, Chanthika Pornpitakpan found that Americans should adapt their behaviors when selling to Japanese and Thais, to be more consistent with their cultural expectations. She found that, to achieve better outcomes, American selling to Thais should wear a Thai suit (i.e. Chut Phra Rachatan), accept invitations to lunch, address the client as "Khun" followed by his or her first name, and use less expressive gestures. Likewise, when Americans are selling to Japanese, they should use the Japanese style of exchanging business cards, spend time building the relationship before doing business, and address the client by the title "Buchoo."[13] As a cultural orientation, people who are high in cultural adaptation strive to effectively "blend in" wherever they go in the world. Before traveling, they will often go out of their way to learn cultural norms (and often many words and phrases in the local language). Cultural adaptors believe that there are many ways of accomplishing tasks globally and that the most effective is to try to adapt one's behaviors to fit the given cultural situation or the local context.

The downside of cultural adaptation (especially in the absence of the other cultural orientations) is the potential to over-interpret behaviors on the basis of cultural expectations or nationality. Cultural adaptors can sometimes derail because they are ineffective enacting higher order goals and spend an inordinate amount of time working to be accepted at the local level. At worst, they may even be seen as "phony" or inauthentic in trying to be too much like a member of the local culture.

4.4.3   Cultural Integration

Cultural integration is an orientation to understand the cultural differences of each person in a multicultural or cross-cultural context – but strive to create something that is a combination of many cultural perspectives. Cultural integrators are especially well-suited for situations requiring a new policy, practice, or project to be created through the input of many diverse perspectives. For example, cultural integrators can make very effective global team leaders because they will invest the time at the onset to develop operating procedures all team members can accept. Cultural integrators are able to effectively create operational assimilation wherever they go in the world. Cultural integrators believe that the best solution is usually developed from a variety of opinions and perspectives.

The downside of cultural integration (especially in the absence of the other two cultural orientations) is the potential to take too much time building consensus and acceptable process, especially in situations where the company's approach (or local approach) would work just as well. Cultural integrators can sometimes derail because they are ineffective enacting company-wide goals and/or are not operating through local norms when they are needed. Cultural integrators are often frustrated with centrally controlled and highly localized policies and practices.

The culturally agile professionals are able to operate with each of the three cultural orientations, depending on the demands of the professional situation: They will leverage the behaviors of a cultural minimalist when the situation demands that their behaviors supersede the local context. They will adapt their behaviors when the situation demands attention to the local context. They will create a new behavioral set, taking elements from multiple cultural contexts.

There are a variety of methods companies can use to develop culturally agile individuals within organizations who can quickly, successfully, and comfortably assess cross-cultural situations and appropriately adapt based on the needs of the cultural and business context. In Chapter 6 we will discuss the selection, training, and development practices human resources can leverage to produce a better pipeline of managers and individual contributors who are culturally agile.

4.5 Human Resource Practices and Cultural Differences

From these themes, we can imagine the many possible implications cross-cultural difference may have when managing the global workforce, especially on HR practices. As discussed in Chapter 2, companies approach their global HR systems from the same three perspectives that culturally agile leaders do. Companies can export HR practices, adapt HR practices, and integrate HR practices. Just as the most culturally agile people decide when to use each of the three approaches for managing cultural differences, global firms should do the same with respect to the decisions of HR practices. As Chapter 2 described, the answers to the following three questions should help guide when to export, adapt, or integrate a given practice in order to align with necessary strategic capabilities. The three questions are:

1 What is necessary at the firm level to be consistent around the world and how should that consistency be managed or controlled across the workforce? To answer this question we need to first determine the non negotiable or common factors (e.g. ethical behaviors, safety behaviors, and quality craftsmanship) upon which the company competes. Once determined, what is the HR system or what are the specific human resource management practices for attracting, retaining, developing, and motivating employees to produce this common factor? How can the practice be exported

so similar behaviors are produced across the various foreign subsidiaries in order to achieve uniformity around the world? Exporting HR practices can be challenging because they may be asking individuals to engage in counter-culture behaviors. If this is the case, there are three general sets of HR practices available to achieve this:

(a) by reinforcing certain behaviors (while punishing or not rewarding others) as a condition for continued employment, promotion, bonus, etc. Over time, people who can adapt to counter-culture behaviors will remain with the organization while others will leave (voluntarily or involuntarily);

(b) by attempting to change behaviors through training and development and reinforcing in a culturally acceptable manner by working within local norms to effect a change (e.g. allow for training to be conducted in a local language or explained in a locally acceptable way). Over time the behavior will be consistent but the means of getting there may be different; and

(c) by hiring those people who are atypical of the culture or already display the needed counter-culture behaviors. Over time, depending on the firm's reputation, those with the necessary counter-culture behaviors may be more attracted to working for the firm and may be more likely to be selected by the firm.

2 **What is necessary at the firm level to vary around the world and how should that localization be managed within each subsidiary?** To answer this question we need to first determine the factors (e.g. reliable distribution, cost-effective operations, and elite product image) upon which the company competes in the local environment. Once determined, what is the HR system or what are the specific human resource management practices for attracting, retaining, developing, and motivating employees to achieve this factor within each subsidiary? How can HR practices be adapted or developed internally within subsidiaries to maximize their success within each of the foreign subsidiaries? It is relatively straightforward to develop these HR practices because each subsidiary is acting independently; these practices, however, should be evaluated for their success at achieving the expected results locally.

3   What is necessary at the firm level to be shared among the firm's foreign subsidiaries and with headquarters? If we want subsidiaries to cooperate with one another, as well as with headquarters, which HR practices will facilitate this cooperation and what will impede such cooperation? What are the factors critical for the firm's success that warrant this level of integration and shared cooperation (e.g. research and development, operational systems)? HR practices may include any training and development to improve communications and cooperation cross-nationally. This may include structured opportunities for geographically dispersed associates to convene and create the sense of a common goal or purpose.

4.6   Chapter Conclusions

This chapter has explored cultural differences and encourages you to consider the following when managing the global workforce.

Learn about cultural differences. When you visit different countries or interact with people from different cultures, try to observe the behaviors that may be culturally based. Ask questions and listen. Read about the target culture. Engage with cultural training tools to explore differences that you experience to better understand the values-based cross-national roots. Once you have a deep understanding of a given cultural difference, consider how such differences may affect individuals' work behaviors and attitudes.

Understand how cultural differences will influence how you manage in the global workforce. Cultural differences will influence how you gain credibility, communicate effectively, and work with people from diverse cultures. These not only affect the acceptance or use of HR practices but they also affect how well you will work with people from different cultures and manage cross-culturally.

Be culturally agile. Understanding cultural differences is not enough when managing the global workforce. Once cultural differences are fully understood (and observed), consider how best to manage them given the strategic necessity of the business. In some cases it is best to minimize or override the cultural differences. In other cases you may need to adapt to the cultural norms. At times it may be best to acknowledge multiple perspectives and try to create something new which is not consistent with either set of cultural norms.

Understand the influence of cultural difference on the acceptance of HR practices. Based on the strategic capabilities desired by a given firm, companies can export HR practices, adapt HR practices, and integrate HR practices. Within the same firm, there may be strategic reasons to export certain practices, while adapting or integrating other practices.

Notes

1 Cultural agility was first introduced by Dr Paula Caligiuri in 2007. The assessment for cultural agility is *The Self-Assessment for Global Endeavors*. RW-3: New York.

2 Source of *NY Times* quote about Howard Stringer: "Man In The News: A Career of Crossing Cultures for Sony's New Boss" by Bill Carter. Published March 7, 2005. Accessed October 28, 2007 at http://www.nytimes.com/2005/03/07/business/worldbusiness/07stringer.html.

3 Cultural agility is first defined in: Caligiuri, P. and Tarique, I. "Developing managerial and organizational cross-cultural capabilities", invited book chapter in Cary Cooper and Ron Burke (eds), *The Peak Performing Organization* (Routledge Publishers, 2008).

4 Sony's Boogie Knight Sir Howard Stringer is on a quest. To battle the media giants, he must connect Sony's content to its magical electronics devices. By Marc Gunther, March 19, 2001, http://www.cnnmoney. com.

5 Triandis, H. C., *Culture and Social Behavior* (McGraw-Hill, 1994).

6 Hofstede, G., *Culture's Consequences* (Beverly Hills: Sage, 1980). Hofstede, G., *Cultures and Organizations: Software of the Mind* (McGraw-Hill, 1991).

7 Hofstede, G., Culture's Consequences: International Differences in Work-Related Values (Sage, 1980).

8 Hofstede, G., *Cultures and Organizations: Software of the Mind* (McGraw-Hill, 1991); Hall, E. T., (1960). The Silent Language in Overseas Business. *Harvard Business Review*, May–June; Trompenaars, A. and Hampden-Turner, C., *The Seven Cultures of Capitalism* (Doubleday, 1993); Kluckhohn, F. and Strodtbeck, F.L., *Variations in Value Orientations* (Row, Peterson, 1961).

9 Hall, E. T., *Beyond Culture* (New York: Anchor/Doubleday, 1971). Hall, E. T., *The Dance of Life. The Other Dimension of Time* (New York: Doubleday, 1983).

10 Expedia.com – 2008 International Vacation Deprivation™ Survey Results, Harris Interactive survey. Accessed September 20, 2008 at http://media.expedia.com/media/content/expus/graphics/promos/vacations/expedia_international_vacation_deprivation_survey_2008.pdf.

11 IKEA Press Release. IKEA Seeking 400 to Join Swedish Family in University City: Recruitment Underway for Store Opening Spring 2009 in Charlotte, NC. October 26, 2008.

12 August 18, 2008. Getting it Right: Pret A Manger. *The Insider.*

13 Pornpitakpan, C. (1999). The Effects of Cultural Adaptation on Business Relationships: Americans Selling to Japanese and Thais. *Journal of International Business Studies*, 2nd qtr, 30(2): 317–337.

CHAPTER 5

Global Workforce
Planning

The Global Mobility of People,
Jobs, and Knowledge

5.1 Offshoring and Dell:
An Illustrative Example

Given the vast differences in labor supply and demand, wage rates, and skill sets around the world, many companies have explored a number of potential "offshore" locations to assume business activities. From a cost perspective, offshoring has great potential to help reduce fixed costs and keep prices for customers, as well as profits of companies, at attractive levels. And with access to a ready supply of capable workers, companies are able to ensure they have the necessary talent in place to meet their business needs. One company that has experienced success with offshoring, as well as some troubles, is Dell.

Dell Computer Company is a leading provider of desktop and notebook computers in the United States and elsewhere in the world. As noted on their corporate website,[1] every Fortune 100 company does business with Dell and Dell has been the number one PC supplier to small and large enterprises throughout the United States for 10 straight years. With this kind of success, it is not surprising that they ship about 140 000 systems every day. And with this type of demand, it is understandable that they have nearly 2 billion interactions with their customers each year. The 2 billion interactions with customers are an important point to consider with regard to the use of offshoring customer service at Dell. Customer relations is an important part of Dell's longstanding reputation with companies and consumers, and with this many interactions, it is important to maintain a high level of satisfaction with customers to help sustain that reputation as a high service provider. Unfortunately, Dell experienced some backlash from customers regarding the offshoring of some call centers and, as a result, they have reassessed their offshoring strategies and moved some of their call center support back to the US.[2]

This reassessment of offshoring is not limited to Dell. Companies such as US Airways, HSBC, Powergen, and the Royal Bank of Scotland have taken steps to bring home some of their past offshoring decisions. Some of these companies even use these decisions in their marketing – reminding customers that their support is provided within country. Given the potential cost savings with offshoring, the logical question is, why the change? For one, some customers complained about language barriers and quality of support. Another reason, however, is that the savings do not necessarily always outweigh the costs. One study by CFI group found that customer satisfaction was 23 % less for overseas call center support than for US call centers. The reasons may vary considerably, but the reality is that there is a trend for customer assessment of offshore service to be lower than when the service is within country.[3]

In response to these concerns, many companies have begun to rethink their offshoring strategies as part of their global workforce planning. One technique that has gained some momentum across companies is to adopt a multisource approach. In this approach some types of calls are routed to one location while other calls are routed to other countries. For instance, HSBC bank and British Airways now offer British call centers for clients wanting detailed financial or travel advice, while maintaining their Indian call centers for low-end queries.[4] But Dell has taken this a step further. In December 2008, Dell announced a new service plan for its customers called "Your Tech Team." As noted on their website, Your Tech Team is a new concept that allows consumers to have access to a preferred technical support person, a guaranteed response of less than two minutes, and access to North American support rather than support from India and the Philippines.[5] Of course, there is a catch. To have this support customers must be willing to pay a monthly or yearly fee.[6]

This discussion of offshoring at Dell and other companies raises a number of interesting and important questions. For example, why is there backlash with offshoring? Is it only about the service or is there something deeper? How can companies ensure that their offshore locations provide quality support and customers remain happy with the support they receive? Is it reasonable to charge for customer support, as Dell has initiated recently, to customers that may already expect that level of support as part of the purchase of the products? Many companies are struggling to develop a global workforce strategy that helps them sustain or enhance their competitiveness in industry. The focus of this chapter is to explore the options for developing such a global workforce strategy.

5.2 Global Workforce Planning

In the previous chapters we focused on three foundational areas for managing a global workforce. In Chapter 2 we explored strategic levers and the ways in which human resource practices may vary depending on the strategic goals of the transnational firm. We also addressed questions such as: How does human talent affect international integration, local responsiveness, and worldwide innovation and collaboration? In Chapter 3 we explored differences in countries' HR systems that are relevant when transnational firms operate in multiple foreign countries, adding to the complexity of managing a global workforce. This chapter explored questions such as: What are the cross-border differences in employment and labor laws, workforce competence (e.g. literacy rates and educational systems), labor economics, and unionization? In Chapter 4 we focused on cross-cultural differences, describing the cultural dimensions that influence the acceptance of global human resource practices, such as cross-cultural differences in management styles, time, communication, and the like. We explored questions such as: What are the cross-national differences in the ways individuals gain trust and credibility, communicate, and work together?

In the next three chapters we make a transition into the second half of Global Dimensions of Human Resource Management. In these chapters we will examine how the three foundational areas influence three key practice areas of HRM: global workforce planning, managing competencies, and managing attitudes and behaviors. The focus of this chapter is on global workforce planning.

The importance of global workforce planning rests on the basic argument that with advances in technology and information systems, supply chain logistics, and educational developments, companies are able to operate in a truly global manner. While this certainly implies selling products and delivering services around the globe, it also means thinking about a global workforce strategy. But what exactly does a global workforce strategy imply? A useful way to think about this question is to consider three points.

First, global workforce planning embraces the notion of a global mobility of people. This concept is certainly not new in multinational corporations, but reinforces the fact that companies are able to send their own employees around the world to work in their subsidiaries, and that they are able to hire people from host countries or third countries to work for them in various locations. When people think about global workforce planning, this focus on expatriates, expatriates, host country nationals, and third country nationals is what most of us are familiar with.

Second, beyond the mobility of people, global workforce planning also embraces the possibility of the global mobility of jobs. This notion of sending jobs, rather than people, to locations around the globe has increased in prominence in recent years with the increased use of offshoring by organizations. With the global mobility of jobs, companies are open to the notion that work can be performed by anyone, anywhere in the world.

The third point of global workforce planning is the concept of a global mobility of knowledge. The mobility of people and jobs still involves physical proximity to work. However, the global mobility of knowledge embraces the possibility of people working together, sharing their knowledge and expertise from around the world to enhance the performance of the locations as well as the multinational corporation. This can involve sending people to other countries to work in specific locations, or sending work to people already in those locations.

These three components of global workforce planning – the global mobility of people, jobs, and knowledge – form the three key components that are involved with developing a global workforce strategy. Let's discuss these now.

5.3   Global Mobility of People

Populating the worldwide organizational structure of every multinational firm are employees who collectively constitute the global workforce. Every employee, and potential employees, within the global workforce has a country of *location* (where he or she lives and works) and a country of *nationality* (where he or she is from). With respect to nationality, employees within the total global workforce may share nationality with their employing transnational organization (domestic workforce) or may have a different nationality from their employing transnational (host national or foreign workforce). The proportion of domestic and foreign employees can vary tremendously, often relative to the size of the domestic market. With respect to location, employees may be living and working in their home country or may be living away from their home country in a foreign country. These two dimensions, nationality and location, provide a matrix to better understand transnational firms' total global workforce, as all employees fit into any one of five categories: domestic employees, host national employees, expatriates, inpatriates, and third country nationals. Table 5.1 graphically depicts this categorization.

Domestic employees live and work in the same national location as the headquarters for their firm. Americans working for IBM, Mexicans working for Cemex, and Japanese working for Sony are all examples of domestic employees. These employees do not need to work at headquarters, merely to share nationality and national location with their headquarters. *Host national workers* live and work in their country of origin, but work for a company that is headquartered in another country. Americans working for Sony or Cemex in the United States, Mexicans working for Sony or IBM in Mexico, and Japanese working for IBM or Cemex in Japan are all examples of host national employees. *Expatriates* share nationality with their headquarters country and are sent to a foreign country to live and work. Americans working for IBM in Mexico, Mexicans working for Cemex in Japan, and Japanese working for Sony in the United States are all examples of expatriates. A variation of expatriate employees is *inpatriate* employees, host national employees who move into the headquarters country to live and work for a period of time.

Table 5.1 Categorization of the Global Workforce

		Location of the Position	
		In the country where HQ is located	*In a host national or foreign subsidiary*
Nationality of Employee	Same nationality as the HQ country	Domestic Employee	Expatriate
	Different nationality from HQ country but the same as the country where the position is located		Host National Employee
	Different nationality from HQ country and different from the country where the position is located	Inpatriate	Third Country National

Americans working for Sony in Japan, Mexicans working for IBM in the United States, and Japanese working for Cemex in Mexico are all examples of inpatriates. *Third country nationals* are those employees who do not share nationality with either their headquarters country or the country where they are living and working. Examples of third country nationals would include Japanese employees working for IBM in Mexico and Americans working for Sony in Mexico.

Multinational firms typically have a mix of these domestic, host national, expatriate, inpatriate, and third country nationals and ultimately need to be able answer two questions: (1) Who do we have where? (2) And why? The answer to the first question is a descriptive understanding of the five categories of employees constituting any given firm's global workforce. The latter affects far more strategic issues, such as the extent to which leaders are developed across geographies, the extent to which headquarters will maintain control over foreign subsidiaries, the extent to which geographical or cross-national teams will need to share information, the extent to which low value-added jobs can be moved to lower labor-cost countries, and the tradeoffs associated with each role.

At a basic level, we can think of the potential returns of each category of global worker in terms of a multinational company's strategic goals for local responsiveness relative to global efficiency.

Host country nationals, for example, might be best positioned for achieving local responsiveness. From a cost perspective, they are likely to have the greatest labor supply for an international subsidiary job assignment. In the host location, the greatest number of available employees will most likely be locals. And given their familiarity with the local region and the cultural preferences, tastes, styles, and norms of the country, the amount and types of training necessary for cultural integration are limited. Consider the necessary training for an expatriate employee in comparison to a local. Aside from the compensation costs of expatriates, getting them ready to move and work in a foreign location can be quite expensive. In contrast, the use of host country nationals helps keep the costs down relative to other categories of workers. But from a strategic point of view, there are also clear benefits of these workers. Namely, their intimate knowledge of the local region, of customers, suppliers, and distributors, and of how business is conducted, which is very valuable for helping ensure smooth operations.

In contrast, when the focus is on global efficiency, expatriates might prove particularly effective. With a global strategy, companies are not aligned with a particular country, nor do they target the unique tastes and preferences of individual countries. Rather, they strive to align business units across countries to realize gains in efficiency and scope. Because expatriate job assignments are situations in which parent company employees are assigned to work in subsidiaries located in a host country, they offer a set of particular benefits, benefits that are particularly valuable for a global efficiency strategy. For example, they are uniquely positioned to transfer corporate values and technological know-how, or to facilitate diffusion of innovative practices and processes to the subsidiary location. In addition, they may help socialize location-specific managers to better understand and adopt the values and procedures of the multinational corporation. And while the use of expatriates might involve considerable expense,[7] the likelihood of success for increased global efficiencies in these contexts is likely to be greater for expatriates than for host country nationals, third country nationals, and inpatriates, none of which have the same level of knowledge of the parent company operations and norms.

When companies are pursuing both global efficiency and local responsiveness, an increased reliance on inpatriates may be very effective. Because inpatriates are trained in the parent location they are socialized into the corporate culture and understand the competitive pressures and needs of the organization. Moreover, they are able to share their knowledge of the host culture with the headquarters staff, a tactic that can facilitate learning for future activities. And because they are intimately familiar with the host location, they are a valuable asset in navigating the cultural, social, political, and competitive landscape of the local environment. As a result, inpatriates are uniquely positioned with understanding both the country culture and the company culture, norms, routines, and demands.[8]

As this discussion indicates, the global mobility of people reflects the potential tactic of moving people around the world to facilitate the effective operation of subsidiaries and the parent multinational corporation. It should be obvious that with each type of worker, however, there are clear advantages and disadvantages for MNCs. For example, expatriates are great for standardization of operations around the world, transmitting corporate values and procedures, and socializing managers in subsidiary locations. However, they are quite costly. Similar tradeoffs exist for inpatriates, domestic employees, host country, and third country nationals. Given these tradeoffs, a more appropriate way to think about the global mobility of people is to focus on the strategic needs of the MNC and the subsidiary locations and to identify which type of worker is most likely to enable the realization of those strategic objectives. As we discussed, the best choice depends on the circumstances.

5.4   Global Mobility of Jobs

The global mobility of jobs refers to the ability of companies to move work such as a single job or entire functions, departments, units or enterprises almost anywhere in the world. While the global mobility of people is focusing on moving people around the world to where they can add the most value, the global mobility of jobs is different – it is viewing the world as a global labor market and deciding where work should be performed. In this discussion, many companies have increasing their interest in or reliance on *offshoring* –

sending work that was once performed domestically to companies in other countries, or opening facilities in other countries to do the work, often at a substantially lower cost.[9] Oracle has 2000 employees in India,[10] and Levi's has closed all of its plants in the United States to focus operations in other countries.[11] In a 2007 survey of 500 fast growing companies, Deloitte found that 45% are currently using offshore firms and 55% plan to use them in the next five years.[12] Whether it is Indian workers preparing US tax returns or staffing call centers for Dell or AOL in India, offshoring has emerged as a major strategic tactic that is available for companies to use.

Of course, it is important to realize that there are advantages and disadvantages with offshoring. The most common advantages noted are costs savings, access to labor, and the ability to modify the workday through round-the-clock shift work and follow-the-sun strategies. There are, however, disadvantages as well that must be considered. Let's view these in more detail.

5.4.1 Cost Savings

When we discuss offshoring, the primary reason that comes to mind for most professionals and executives is cost savings. In Chapter 3 we discuss how countries vary dramatically with regard to their labor costs and labor supply as well as the level and types of skills they have among their human capital. These differences have fueled the offshoring trend. For some firms, the availability of a large labor supply in another country, coupled with potentially lower labor costs in those nations, is a very attractive option for staffing multinational operations. For example, a call center worker costs an employer roughly $ 30–60 per hour in the US. The same work can be performed in China for $ 13–15, in India for $ 13–18, and in the Czech Republic for between $ 25–32. These are certainly labor cost savings. Given these considerations, it should not be surprising that US companies such as American Standard have set up operations in countries like Bulgaria, where wages are a fraction of what they are in the United States.[13] According to the McKinsey Global Institute, companies save $ 0.58 for every dollar of spending on jobs in India. Similarly, German companies save 0.52 euros for every euro of corporate spending they offshore to India.[14] Even the wages in

Table 5.2   Labor Costs in Central Europe

Country	Factory Worker	Engineer	Accountant	Middle Manager
Poland	$ 3.07	$ 4.32	$ 4.03	$ 6.69
Czech Republic	$ 2.81	$ 5.38	$ 4.10	$ 6.81
Hungary	$ 1.96	$ 5.09	$ 4.62	$ 7.44
Slovakia	$ 2.21	$ 4.15	$ 3.37	$ 5.48
Romania	$ 1.41	$ 2.58	$ 1.23	$ 3.23
Bulgaria	$ 0.73	$ 1.43	$ 0.83	$ 2.80
Germany	$ 18.80	$ 38.90	$ 26.40	$ 40.40

Source: Ewing, J. and Edmondson, G. December 12, 2005. The rise of Central Europe. *Business Week*, pp. 50–56.

countries in close proximity to one another (those in Central Europe, for example) range widely, as Table 5.2 shows.

Consider the potential for cost savings on a broader scale. Hypothetically, if a company offshored accounting work from Germany to Bulgaria, they would realize a savings of $ 25.57 per hour. If one employee worked 2000 hours over the year, that would be a saving of $ 51 140. If this company offshored 10 jobs doing this work, that would result in over half a million dollars in savings. While these wage rates are clearly dramatically different, even when the rates are closer, the savings add up. Consider outsourcing from Poland to Hungary for a factory worker. The difference in hourly wage is $ 1.17. For 2000 hours per year, that is a saving of $ 2340.00. If that factory had 100 workers, this would generate a saving on labor costs of $ 234 000.00. Though purely hypothetical, these examples demonstrate the attractiveness of the potential costs savings associated with offshoring work.

5.4.2   Access to Talent

While the most frequently noted reason for offshoring is cost savings, an additional key motivator is access to qualified personnel. Given the global race for talent, it is not surprising that managers are exploring pockets around the world to serve as a supply source for talented workers. The average education level of the workforce, the occupational background, and the supply of workers with different skill sets varies dramatically from country to country. Regions in China and India, for instance, have experienced a boom in global demand for work and a source for new operations from multinational corporate around the world. In part this is because the labor costs in these regions lag behind the costs in many of the multinational home locations. However, it is also because the pure volume of supply of workers with adequate skills, if not outstanding skills, makes these locations particularly desirable. For example, Bangalore, India has emerged as a cluster of talent for IT and software skills, while Moscow and St. Petersburg have emerged as desirable talent locations for highly trained scientists.[15] A study by the Offshoring Resource Network found that almost 50% of all IT and product development offshore projects were implemented in India.[16] Given the talent available, it shouldn't be surprising that companies such as Texas Instruments, General Electric, Motorola, and Daimler have established technology centers in India.

Sometimes the desirable locations are not cheap at all, but potentially expensive. One interesting example exists in the fashion industry:

> Milan, Italy is certainly not known for its low production costs, yet most fashion houses have a design office there to take advantage of the knowledge and skills at the hub of the fashion world. Being there allows them to gauge fashion trends and profit from the world-class talent pool.[17]

If we view the world as a potential workforce, it is not surprising that different regions have different levels and types of talent. Some regions have a surplus of scientists and researchers while others have a shortage. Some regions have specialized knowledge while others do not. And while costs may certainly be a consideration, it may also be the case that the labor force in another country excels in certain areas of expertise such as science or medicine, or simply has a greater supply of labor for a particular expertise.[18] As this example shows, access to expertise is an important consideration when considering the global mobility of work. And sometimes the costs are actually greater with offshoring, but the benefit is the ability to reach a pocket of talent needed for competitive success.

5.4.3 Round the Clock Shifts

An additional potential benefit of offshoring jobs relates to operational efficiency gains. Although offshoring may present challenges in terms of distance and coordinating with vendors or employees scattered around the world, it also presents an opportunity for operating your firm "24/7" – operating without any downtime. A partner of a US firm in India, for example, may conceivably start its workday just as the employees in the US are completing their workday. Take the call center industry. By relying on staffing around the world, call centers can be fully staffed at all times of the day. When it is daytime in the US, calls are routed to US call centers. As the sun sets in the US, and rises in India, calls can be routed to Indian call centers. Because the time difference is 12.5 hours, call centers in India can be just starting to work for the day while the offices in the US are just closing. Given the potential for no downtime, the Mc Kinsey Global Institute suggests that simply increasing the number of shifts may result in a 30–44% reduction in operating costs for many types of offshore work.[19] Considering the importance of quick and responsive customer service, it is appealing to companies to be able to provide this level of support.

5.4.4 Follow the Sun

Closely related to round the clock staffing, follow-the-sun strategies enable companies to have a workforce working on projects around the clock. One subtle difference, however, is that the focus is not simply on keeping the office open; rather, it is on continuing the production process to avoid stops and starts. When a worker in one region of the world has finished working on a project they can send their work in progress to another employee located halfway around the world. The second employee then spends their day working on the project, while the first employee is off duty. By doing so, companies are able to decrease the time it takes to create products or services while dramatically increasing their firms' labor pools.

Of course, this strategy might not be possible for physical production of products, but for knowledge work that can be shared via technology, it is a viable option to consider. Given the continual pressures firms are under to bring out new products faster than their competitors and at lower costs, it is logical that companies such as General Electric, Citigroup, and American Express continue to expand their offshoring operations.[20]

5.4.5 Offshoring Risks

As a result of offshoring, countries around the world are being evaluated as potential locations for establishing offshore operations. Although the United States has witnessed an increasing trend towards the offshoring of its manufacturing jobs, more recently we have witnessed the offshoring of professional and white-collar jobs, too. For example, many IT jobs, call center positions, and back office operations are being offshored to India, Eastern Europe, and the Philippines.[21] The low labor costs coupled with the necessary human capital that is needed to do the job (e.g. competency in spoken English) make these locations attractive for many organizations that try to achieve global economies of scale. As we have seen earlier in this discussion, it is obvious that there are some compelling potential benefits.

However, cost savings are not the entire story. In fact, other costs associated with poor service, lost customers, poor collaboration, and the like may actually outweigh the benefits of offshoring. One survey found that roughly two-thirds of US customers would consider reducing their purchases or cease all purchases from companies who offshore customer service support.[22] As indicated in this chapter's opening case, Dell stopped routing technical support calls from US customers to a call center in Bangalore, India, because customers complained about the service.[23] Companies must balance their cost savings with achieving the strategic objectives they are trying to achieve such as improved product quality, customer service, and the like.[24] It is imperative to ensure that offshoring your business processes and activities does not alienate your customers or compromise the quality of your operations. Saving costs at the expense of other performance outcomes is unlikely to be a sustainable strategy over time.[25]

Another potential cost relates to turnover. Turnover at the offshore location may dilute the quality of the workers over time or increase the costs to sustain a similar level of talent through training and/or compensation. It might be a cost saving at first in terms of the average cost per hour for foreign labor. But, if turnover is high, and the level of performance is at all diminished, the actual return per hour of pay might be better for domestic wages than for foreign wages.

There are also concerns that foreign workers may not be functionally fluent in business acumen and customer service. Understanding the language is not the same as understanding how language is used in different cultures, how formal or informal discussions should be, and how business conversations are expected to unfold. The Royal Bank of Scotland and NatWest are two companies that ran advertisements that they moved their call centers back to Britain. They are banking on the fact that consumers will be happier with this decision than the potential costs savings that existed in offshore locations. Of course, this doesn't mean these companies are not offshoring jobs, it just means the jobs being offshored do not require the same level of customer contact. In this regard, it is important to recognize that offshoring is not viable for many jobs, especially jobs with a high level of customer interaction.

Aside from the strategic rationale, there are also potential social concerns stemming from consumer backlash about the ethics of offshoring. While offshoring is a logical option to consider for a global workforce strategy, some people within a society may view offshoring as a bad company practice. This sentiment is not based on strategic rationales for the company success but from a social perspective. Offshoring is viewed by some as taking jobs away from friends, family, and others within one's country.

Finally, even if companies are able to realize all of these benefits, a concern regards its investment for the future. If we focus on the issue of which employee talent pools drive value creation within organizations, a question remains as to whether these jobs should be offshored at all. If they are critical for competitive advantage, offshoring them might potentially realize short-term benefits, but it also might result in long-term compromises to a company's strategic position. Put simply, if you offshore jobs that are strategically critical and help set you apart, what is left to set you apart from your competitors and to prevent your offshoring partner from becoming a competitor?

In sum, we suggest that there is a strong incentive for companies to consider offshoring jobs that:

■ are not strategically critical;
■ may be performed at a lower cost in another country;
■ are supported by a viable organization in that country to deliver that task or service.

By doing so, the company may be able to recoup those costs, access greater efficiencies and/or expertise in the performance of the tasks by the offshoring provider, and divert their investments to more value-added core employees. In these scenarios, offshoring is a logical extension of more traditional domestic-based outsourcing or contractual arrangements. However, it must be done with the potential disadvantages of offshoring in mind.

5.5 Global Mobility of Knowledge

The global mobility of knowledge refers to the notion that people from anywhere in the world can work together anywhere, anytime, for anyone. Not too long ago companies were bounded by proximity – employees had to work near their offices. Companies recruited locally to staff operations or sent their own employees to staff those operations (global mobility of people). Over time, companies explored the mobility of people – they sent people to many locations and explored ways to maximize the return on international assignments. Or, companies established operations in locations with sufficient talent to run the business (global mobility of jobs).

The global mobility of knowledge pushes these boundaries and requires that managers think about who knows what, where they are, and how to leverage that knowledge for competitive success. What this means is that it is more than just moving people and jobs, it is about tapping expertise around the globe in ways that are more fluid and flexible. It is about finding high performers that can fill positions or contribute knowledge on a temporary basis that may be dispersed throughout the world. It is finding ways of connecting individuals who possess key talent wherever they are located, placing them in the right position, and letting them deliver. It is about maximizing the knowledge creation of your employees and tapping the knowledge of people who don't even work for you, or only do so on a part time basis.

Historically, HR has been grounded in the job. This is mostly a relic of the profession's development in the era of large-scale manufacturing. But the business environment has changed. Increasingly, the knowledge that companies rely on for competitive success resides not only in the minds of their employees who are proximally located, but also in the minds of contractors, consultants, and other external workers with whom they collaborate.

While a central challenge for companies that compete based on knowledge is to have a clear sense of what knowledge their employees presently hold and need in order to achieve the organization's business goals, it is equally important to promote exchange of knowledge, innovation, and learning to maintain competitive distinction. That is, it is not knowledge per se that makes a competitive edge possible, but rather the extent to which the company can effectively manage knowledge to create value over time. This distinction reflects the difference between managing jobs around the globe and managing the flow of knowledge among employees and between employees and partners.[26] Given the challenges associated with managing information among relevant parties in MNCs, there are several tactics that are of use, including transnational teams, virtual teams, and partnership or network-based structures.

5.5.1   Transnational Teams

With a complex multinational corporation, the difficulties of coordinating and integrating information around the world and across locations increase dramatically. In part, this is a function of the reality that organizations are organic and evolve with changes in the competitive landscape. One subsidiary in Eastern Europe evolves as the competitive circumstances evolve. Likewise, subsidiaries in Southeast Asia evolve to cope with and navigate changes in those circumstances. While it is challenging in its own right for each unit to cope with its respective location, think about the challenges with coordinating across these units which are always evolving.

In classical management theory there is a notion that when it comes to organizational structure, the more an organization differentiates to cope with the environment, the more integration is needed to function effectively. In multinational corporations, the importance of differentiation is critical to allow for local responsiveness. From the corporation perspective, however, the need for integration is equally high.

Transnational teams are one means to share knowledge and information across subsidiaries and international locations to help the broader multinational corporation function effectively. Transnational teams are groups of people from different cultures brought together on activities that span national borders.[27] These teams often comprise leaders from different subsidiaries, with different functional backgrounds and different experiences. With such a diverse set of background traits and experiences, transnational teams are positioned to address a variety of different types of issues.

With such a structure, the goal is that these teams help their firms be flexible enough for the different subsidiaries to be locally responsive, while at the same time learning from one another to develop the efficiencies needed for global integration. Of course, the relative emphasis placed on local responsiveness and/or global integration can vary. Some transnational teams are assembled to learn how better to respond to the unique needs of different regions. Other teams are assembled to identify ways to increase integration across operations in different regions. Beyond these two objectives, many transnational teams have an explicit objective of organizational learning,[28] to share information that benefits each subsidiary as well as the broader MNC.

There are challenges with relying on transnational teams. For example, success in these teams requires cooperation. This might be difficult to achieve due to language barriers, differences of cultural values and backgrounds, and differences in experiences from different locations.[29] Another challenge relates to the ability to share knowledge effectively and translate it into useful information at the host location. Given differences in the challenges and circumstances across subsidiary locations, it may not really be possible to apply what is learned from the transnational team to all locations equally. Nevertheless, the value is considerable for transnational teams as a mechanism to pull together expertise from different regions of the world, thereby addressing local as well as global problems regarding products, services, operations, or any other business-related activity.

5.5.2 *Virtual Teams*

While the use of transnational teams provides companies with an ability to connect leaders across borders to share information to help the corporation and their own locations, another mechanism that has potential for the global mobility of knowledge is the use of virtual teams. Internet, videoconferencing, and specialized software allow dispersed individuals to collaborate electronically as virtual teams – working together even when they cannot physically be in the same location.[30] Eastman Kodak, Hewlett Packard, General Electric, and Sun Microsystems are just a few of the companies that rely on virtual teams to work on important business objectives.[31]

While virtual teams are a valuable tool in all organizations, the potential benefits are magnified in multinational organizations. The first primary benefit is cost savings. Transnational team use is somewhat limited due to the costs of meeting. You can imagine the costs associated with sending 10 senior leaders from around the world to a single location to meet. The flights and hotel costs alone are too prohibitively expensive to allow face-to-face meetings for many potentially global dispersed teams.

Second, as their name implies, virtual teams do not require face-to-face interaction. There are no delays with coordinating meetings and events; as a result, virtual teams are able to respond quickly to pressing issues, problems, and opportunities. On short notice, individuals may dial into a discussion involving all relevant parties regardless of their respective locations. This flexibility is particularly valuable when problems require solutions that involve know-how from people who are not always in the same place.

Finally, and perhaps the most important, the use of virtual teams dramatically expands who may be part of the team. Virtual team members may be located anywhere in the world – a benefit that is particularly helpful for companies operating on a global scale. One implication is that employees around the globe can work together on a host of issues to help different regions or the corporate headquarters.

Simply establishing virtual teams does not ensure their success. Rather, the organization needs to take several steps to help them realize success. At a basic level, for example, the people involved in the virtual team must have the necessary technology to communicate with other team members. Poor phone connections, incorrect login passwords, incompatible software, difficulties with access to dial into virtual meetings are just some examples of simple problems that confound virtual meetings. Moreover, employees must be trained on how to use the technology.[32] Some additional practices that have been identified for effectively leading virtual teams are:[33]

Establish and maintain trust through the use of communication technology. Managers must focus on developing shared norms regarding how information will be communicated, how technology will be used, and what information may be shared outside of the team.

Ensure that diversity is understood and appreciated. Because members of virtual teams come from a vast array of backgrounds, they typically have a good deal of diversity among the members. It is important for managers to make sure team members are aware of the specific skills of all the other members, and to facilitate ongoing discussions among team members.

Manage virtual work–life cycle and meetings. Just because teams are virtual doesn't mean they have to meet. It just means that how they meet is different. All teams require collaboration and cooperation – otherwise they wouldn't be a team in the first place. Managers in virtual teams need to ensure that virtual meetings take place and are structured to be meaningful and productive.

Monitor team progress using technology. Successful team leaders take advantage of the opportunities of information technologies to monitor the progress of their teams by scrutinizing document postings, electronic threads, virtual meeting participation, instant messaging, and the like.

Enhance visibility of virtual members within the team and its members. Managers must be aware to share information regarding virtual team progress with relevant stakeholders such as project sponsors, executives, and customers of interest. Managers are thus challenged to help work within the team to build a feeling of teamwork while working outside the team as an advocate of the team to others. As team members are often pulled away from their regular work to participate in the virtual teams, it is important for the team leaders to share progress of the team with the member's regular managers so they see the value in sharing their staff with the team.

Enable individual members of the virtual team to benefit from the team. It is also important that virtual team members understand and believe that they are of value to the team and that participating on the team is helpful to them. This can be facilitated through rewards and recognition as well as praise among the team and positive feedback on the employee's performance with their regular manager.

5.5.3   *Network-Based Structures*

Beyond helping employees connect, another form of team, either virtual or proximal, is a team of individual experts that includes both key employees and key external partners or contributors. Many firms are increasing their use of external workers such as temporary employees, independent contractors, consultants, and expert advisors. Proponents of externalization suggest that relying on different forms of external labor may enable firms to be responsive to changes in labor demands, lower labor costs, and increased access to skills their employees do not possess.

These arguments are parallel to the benefits of the tactics discussed above regarding international assignments, offshoring, and teams but go a step forward and consider non-employees as contributors to the organization. For example, while offshoring strives to find pockets around the world to send jobs that might realize cost benefits, tap expert knowledge, or allow 24/7 operations, externalizing work doesn't require the same level of commitment. The externalized arrangements may be with a company or a single person and may be of limited duration or a long-term partnership. This means that, even at a high cost per hour, the costs are only borne when services are provided – achieving significant savings in labor expenses while still accessing expertise.

Related to this is the fact that relying on external labor may also allow firms to realize a decrease in the administrative or bureaucratic overhead associated with managing full time employees. Advocates of outsourcing have long argued that a key saving for organizations relates to personnel expenses such as benefits and training. The added temporal flexibility of these arrangements provides an additional mechanism for MNCs to implement a global workforce strategy. And it is also helpful that companies may partner with experts around the world without having to establish physical operations in those areas – a cost saving that is significant while providing an even greater access to talent around the globe that is not bound by physical limitations or proximity.

One implication for MNCs, however, is that while these employment options are certainly driven by cost considerations, they are also driven by knowledge-based motivations. Often, these external providers are sought for what they know, not just how much they cost. And when this is the case, it raises a need for knowledge exchange. As we have suggested in Chapter 2 and in various portions of this chapter, as organizations become more differentiated to cope with the environment, there is an increased need for integration. Just because some of the people involved in these operations are not employees does not mean this integration isn't needed. What is does mean is that companies must integrate and coordinate with external workers to share knowledge and information for effective functioning.

A key challenge for global mobility of knowledge is not only to have a clear sense of what knowledge its employees presently hold and need in order to achieve business goals, but also to encourage the exchange of knowledge with people who may not even be employees of the organization. The ability to leverage these individuals onto a network-based structure is an additional step toward having a truly global workforce strategy. By integrating individuals with diverse experiences and talents, these different forms of team allow members to examine issues from multiple perspectives that would not be possible by individual employees in isolation. And when teams comprise members with complementary abilities, they may be able to achieve performance levels that exceed the potential of individuals working alone.[34]

Moreover, these team approaches may help improve employee interaction and social support for team members. When people work in disparate locations, the opportunity to interact frequently with others working on common projects and tasks is often welcomed, as it helps individuals maintain their sense of community and involvement in the organization. These are all desirable benefits associated with tactics to manage the global mobility of knowledge.

Of course, there are potential downsides to team-based structures. Teams require high levels of interaction among team members and their success depends directly on the willingness of team members to share their knowledge and ideas. If there is a low degree of trust or insufficient face-to-face interaction, teams may not be able to meet their objectives.[35]

From a practical perspective, it is important to remember that there is great potential with the use of transnational teams, virtual teams, and network structures. Along with those benefits, however, are challenges. The challenges are related to the fact that we are focusing on knowledge exchange rather than simply physical production. We are also focusing on sharing information with nonemployees and depending on nonemployees for success. As we will discuss in Chapters 6 and 7, we have to really think about the best ways to identify the right candidates with the competencies needed for the work and how best to motivate the right attitudes and behaviors through compensation, incentives, and evaluation.

5.6   Chapter Conclusions

Advances in information technology, communication, and educational developments have provided an opportunity for companies to rethink the nature and scope of their workforce. To develop a global workforce strategy, companies need to think about how to manage the global mobility of people, jobs, and knowledge. All these aspects of global workforce planning involve techniques to help organizations increase their ability to reach and leverage talent around the world. By doing so, they are able to access the best and brightest talent in a way that minimizes the costs of doing so. And when tactics are used to help leverage the knowledge among these individuals, multinational corporations are increasingly able to ensure they maintain their ability to be locally responsive and globally efficient. While being a global competitor certainly implies selling products and delivering services around the globe, it also means thinking about a global workforce strategy.

As you strive to adopt a global workforce strategy, consider the following challenges.

Ensure you use the right employment type for your international assignments. There are advantages and disadvantages associated with the use of expatriates, inpatriates, host or third country nationals, or domestic employees. The choice of which employment mode to use should be based on the strategic needs of the MNC and those of the subsidiary locations; it is key to identify which type of worker most likely enables the realization of those strategic objectives. As we discussed, the best choice depends on the circumstances and the goals of the MNC.

The reasons for offshoring will dictate the ideal location. Some regions of the world are more desirable as a source of labor due to their low cost. Mexico and countries in Africa and the Middle East, for example, are often targeted for commodity type work that can be performed at low cost. In contrast, Canada and countries in Western Europe are often targeted for work that is of a much higher skill level. These locations are more viable options for access to high-level talent. The reasons for considering offshoring should dictate where you look for your offshore locations.

Balance ethical tensions. Much of the controversy about offshoring jobs needs to be couched within the context of where the work is done relative to where the products and services are sold. Many firms argue that their international employees are producing for international markets. Critics charge that the international work is too often devised to exploit low-cost labor, with the goods/services being shipped back to the host country. These issues have political as well as competitive implications, and much more research is needed to understand them fully. When we start to think about the loss of jobs from a social and political perspective, we may reach different conclusions than when we view these decisions from a business perspective. These are considerations that must be viewed when making global workforce planning decisions.

Notes

1 Company Facts: Things you should know about Dell. Accessed July 28, 2009 at http://content.dell.com/us/en/corp/d/corp-comm/Company-Facts.aspx.

2 Scott, M., July 25, 2007. Luring customers with local call centers. *Business Week Online*, p. 14. Johnson, M. July 12, 2004. Bracing for backlash. *Computerworld* 38(28): 18.

3 Whoriskey, P., December 11, 2008. The Bangalore Backlash: Call Centers return to U.S. *The Washington Post*, p. D01.

4 Scott, M., July 25, 2007. Luring customers with local call centers. *Business Week Online*, p. 14. Johnson, M., July 12, 2004. Bracing for backlash. *Computerworld* 38(28): 18.

5 Dell Computer Corporation Website. Your Tech Team. Accessed July 28, 2009 at http://www.dell.com/content/topics/segtopic.aspx/services/your_tech_team?c=us&cs=19&l=en&s= dhs.

6 Whoriskey, P., December 11, 2008. The Bangalore Backlash: Call Centers return to U.S. *The Washington Post*, p. D01.

7 Black, J. S., Gregersen, H. B., Mendenhall, M. E., and Stroh, L. K., *Globalizing People through International Assignments* (New York: Addison-Wesley, 1999).

8 Harvey, M. G. (1997). "Inpatriation" training: The next challenge for international human resource management. *International Journal of Intercultural Relations* 21: 393–428.

9 Solomon, C. M. (July 1999). Moving jobs to offshore markets: Why it's done and how it works. *Workforce*. pp. 51–55.

10 Greengard, S., December 2003. What's in Store for 2004. *Workforce.*

11 Serwer, A., October, 13, 2003. Factor Jobs. *Fortune.*

12 Ricci, M., September 10, 2007. Outsourcing 3.0: It's a whole new world, this cost- and quality-control game. *Financial Week.* http://www.financialweek.com.

13 Ewing, J., December 12, 2005. Based in New Jersey, thriving in Bulgaria. *Business Week*, p. 54.

14 Farrell, D., May 2005. Offshoring: Value creation through economic change. *Journal of Management Studies* 42(3): 675–683.

15 Manning, S. Massini, S., and Lewin, A. Y. (2008). A dynamic perspective on next generation offshoring: The global sourcing of science and engineering talent. *Academy of Management Perspectives* 35–54.

16 Ibid.

17 Stringfellow, A., Teagarden, M.B., and Nie, W. (2008). Invisible costs in offshoring services work. *Journal of Operations Management* 26: 164–179.

18 Purcell, J., Purcell, K., and Tailby, S. (2004). Temporary work agencies: Here today, gone tomorrow? *British Journal of Industrial Relations* 42(4): 705–725.

19 Farrell, D., May 2005. Offshoring: Value creation through economic change. *Journal of Management Studies* 42(3): 675–683.

20 Solomon, J., December 6, 2004. India Becomes Collection Hub: Low-Cost Workers Help U.S. Firms Pursue Debtors; Local Companies Go Abroad. *Wall Street Journal*, p. A13.

21 Thibodeau, P., October 18, 2004. Offshoring fuels IT hiring boom in India. *Computerworld*, p. 8; Thottam, J., February 23, 2004. Is your job going abroad? *Time*; Waldman, A., May 11, 2003. More "Can I help you" jobs migrate from U.S. to India. *The New York Times*; Porter, E., June 11, 2004. Not many jobs are sent abroad, U.S. Report says. *The New York Times.*

22 Anton, J. and Setting, T. (2004). The American consumer reacts to the call center experience and the offshoring of service calls. *BenchmarkPortal, Inc.* Stringfellow, A., Teagarden, M. B., and Nie, W. (2008) Invisible costs in offshoring services work. *Journal of Operations Management* 26: 164–179.

23 Brewin, B., December 1, 2003. User complaints push Dell to return PC support to U.S. *Computerworld*; McDougall, P. L. and Claburn, T., December 1, 2003. Offshore 'hiccups in an irreversible trend'. *Information Week.*

24 Aron, R. and Singh, J. V. (2005). Getting offshoring right. *Harvard Business Review*, December, 135–143. Lepak, D. P. and Snell, S. A., "Employment sub-systems and changing forms of employment" in P. Boxall, J. Purcell, and P. Wright (eds), *The Oxford Handbook of Human Resource Management* (Oxford: Oxford University Press, 2007), pp. 210–230.

25 Kripalani, M. January 30, 2006. Five offshore practices that pay off. *Business Week*, pp. 60–61.

26 Boxall, P. (1998). Achieving competitive advantage through human resource strategy: Towards a theory of industry dynamics. *Human Resource Management Review* 8, 265–288; Dierickx, I. and Cool, K. (1989). Asset stock accumulation and sustainability of competitive advantage. *Management Science* 35: 1504–1513; Kang, S. C., Morris, S., and Snell, S. A. (2007) Relational archetypes, organizational learning, and value creation: Extending the human resource architecture. *Academy of Management Review* 32(1): 236–256.

27 Snell, S. A., Snow, C. C., Davison, S. C., and Hambrick, D. C. (1998). Designing and supporting transnational teams: The human resource agenda. *Human Resource Management* 37(2): 147–158.

28 Ibid.

29 Lagerstrom, K. and Andersson, M. (2003). Creating and sharing knowledge within a transnational team – the development of a global business system. *Journal of World Business* 38: 84–95.

30 Kirkman, B. L., Rosen, B., Tesluk, P. E., and Gibson, C. B. (2004). The impact of team empowerment on virtual team performance: The moderating influence of face-to-face interaction. *Academy of Management Journal* 2: 175–192; Lipnack, J. and Stamps, J., *Virtual teams: People working across boundaries with technology*, 2nd edn (New York, NY: John Wiley and Sons Inc., 2000).

31 Ibid.

32 Townsend, A. M., DeMarie, S. M., and Hendrickson, A. R. (1998) Virtual teams: Technology and the workplace of the future. *Academy of Management Executive* 12: 17–29.

33 Malhotra, A., Majchrzak, A., and Rosen, B. (February 2007). Leading virtual teams: Table 1. Practices of effective virtual teams. *Academy of Management Perspectives* 21: 61–70.

34 Zarraga, C. and Bonache, J. (2003). Assessing the team environment for knowledge sharing: An empirical analysis. *International Journal of Human Resource Management* 14: 1227–1245.

35 Kirkman, B. L., Rosen, B., Tesluk, P. E., and Gibson, C. B. (2004). The impact of team empowerment on virtual team performance: The moderating role of face-to-face interaction. *Academy of Management Journal* 47: 175–192.

CHAPTER 6

Managing Competencies

Recruitment, Selection, Training, and Development of the Global Workforce

6.1 Managing Global Safety Behaviors at Shell

Shell has one of the largest logistics operations among oil companies around the world. At Shell, a non-negotiable tenet of the organization in its health and safety practices is a stated goal of zero safety-related injuries. From the Shell website:

> Goal Zero stems from Shell's deeply held value of safety within the business, an initiative which incorporates all employees and contractors and promotes safety and zero harm to our people, and the communities and environment in which we operate.[1]

From Shell's own assessment, 80 % of the safety-related injuries around the world could be prevented if the appropriate behaviors were followed. Collectively, Goal Zero is a tall order for managing human behaviors to a common set of safety norms. For Goal Zero to be effective, Shell has tightly controlled safety practices which allow for no variation, irrespective of culture.

In Shell and any other organization with a safety goal, this example of a relatively straightforward competency, *operating safely*, has human talent challenges when managed globally. For example, *what is objectively defined as safe behavior?* In countries with more fatalistic or risk-taking cultures, one can observe individuals engaging in more risky behaviors (at least by the authors' definition) being taken. When it is deemed necessary to wear hard hats and safety goggles are obvious examples but so are the concerns over having long hair exposed or wearing loose clothing or headscarves near industrial machinery. The former two examples may be easily reinforced behaviors, but the latter examples may require employees to override their cultural norms in order to behave in a way consistent with the company's norms for operating safely.

One approach to managing this competency of operating safely would be to allow each country to operate as they prefer, consistent with their own cultural norms. This is not the case for Shell. When considering a company-level competency, such as operating safely, a globally consistent approach is generally preferred. Culturally agile leaders within organizations like Shell can shape employees' behaviors in a global context using three general approaches: (1) by reinforcing certain behaviors (while punishing or not rewarding others) as a condition for continued employment, promotion, bonus, etc., (2) by attempting to change behaviors through training and development, reinforced in a culturally acceptable manner by working within local norms to affect a change, and (3) by hiring those people who are atypical of the culture or already display the necessary counter-culture behaviors. In most organizations, shaping counter-culture competencies across the global workforce requires a combination of all three approaches. This Shell illustration offers examples of some of these approaches.

Graham Robinson, manager of Shell's Global Zero Work Site Hazard Project, has helped investigate past accidents to ensure future safety at Shell and describes how the company consistently tries to improve safety. He describes the senior leadership of Shell as having an unwavering commitment to safety. Robinson provides evidence of this commitment to Goal Zero at Shell. As part of Goal Zero "a change programme aimed at regions was implemented, and visible recognition for exemplary safety performance and celebration of 'zero days' were carried out. In addition, a zero tolerance policy was adopted for people who create conditions that endanger lives".[2] Showing serious leadership commitment, the zero tolerance policy is one way to override cross-national differences, if any existed; over time, all those who refuse to adapt to the expected norm or behavior will not remain with the organization. For a workforce competence as serious and important as "operating safely" is to Shell, this approach is warranted.

Another, more nuanced, way to manage competencies globally when a common norm is preferred is to work within cultural norms to bring about cultural change. Using the same example, to gain acceptance for Shell's safety program in Indonesia, Darwin Silalahi, Country Chairman and CEO, reiterated the nonnegotiable Shell safety practices and added a collectivist spin, resonating for the group-oriented Indonesians: "At Shell, we believe we are all safety leaders. What each of us does individually results in our collective culture. We must each take personal responsibility for creating a culture of compliance and intervention."[3] Mr. Silalahi was operating with cultural agility as he leveraged knowledge of Indonesian cultural values to institute Shell's nonnegotiable common set of safety practices.

6.2 Managing Competencies in a Global Workforce

Competencies, in the human resource context, are often defined as the combination of knowledge, skills, abilities, and other personal characteristics needed for an individual to successfully perform a task, job, or assignment or succeed, generally, in a given job, role, or position. Operating safely, in the Shell example is an illustration of a competency. Other competencies such as communicating effectively, managing with integrity, motivating associates, providing excellent customer service, negotiating effectively, and the like, vary greatly across jobs, roles, and positions.

Before HR practices are developed to manage workforce competencies, it is important to understand whether there is a strategic necessity to maintain consistency in any given set of employees' competencies across countries or to allow their competencies to vary from country to country, depending on the diverse needs or preferences of the countries. In terms of strategic alignment described in Chapter 2, there are at least three approaches for managing employee competencies across countries. For some competencies, there may be strategic reasons to encourage consistency across those in comparable positions around the world. Shell's Goal Zero (and its associated safety behaviors) is an example of this approach. The more local approach would be for each subsidiary to derive its own competency standards, using its own set of cultural and country-specific norms and preferences.

These strategic decisions regarding global versus local competency standards should drive subsequent HR decisions and practices, influencing the type of people recruited, how they are selected, and how they are trained and developed. In the next section of this chapter we will discuss how human resource practices globally can help manage competencies as a strategic asset for the firm.

6.2.1　Strategic and Global Issues in Employee Attraction and Recruitment

Considering carefully who is brought into the organization is critical to ensure the best talent pipeline is available for the future. It would make logical sense for firms to want to attract the best possible talent, especially for their key positions wherever they operate around the world. Attracting the best possible talent to an organization begs the question: What do employees look for when considering where they want to work – and, when managing the global workforce, does this response differ across cultures? The answers to these questions are critical for recruiting the best possible talent in country locations around the world.

As we know from Chapter 4, cultural differences will include work values cross-nationally. In part, cross-national differences in work values influence how attractive a firm (and its perceived recruitment message) is perceived to be within any given culture because what individuals want from an employer may vary across cultures. Anne-Wil Harzing found differences in individuals' ideal employer image characteristics in business students across 16 European countries. In her study, she reports that students in Eastern European countries generally show different preferences with regard to their ideal employer type than students in other countries, preferring greater money, prestige, and advancement.[4] Cultural differences influence the way in which applicants perceive different dimensions of a prospective employer's recruitment value proposition, what they have to offer their employees.

It is important to first understand your firm's full recruitment message (i.e. why would someone want to work here?) and then consider ways to differentially highlight, or flex, the message across cross-national contexts. For example, in national cultures with a greater balance motivation, vacation time and work–life balance initiatives should be highlighted in the recruitment message. In national cultures that are more collectivist, team work and strong firm identification could be at the front of the recruitment message. In national cultures where responsibility is appreciated, the recruitment message could boast a great leadership development program or advancement opportunities. The same company may offer all of these, but just choose to broadcast different messages depending on the country where they are recruiting talent to be most attractive to key employees within that country. Companies should consider crafting their recruitment message to fit the cultural values of the country where they are recruiting and also encourage their recruiting staff members to tailor their messages to fit the candidates they are trying to attract.

Attracting the best possible talent through tailored recruitment messages is not only desired but also useful given that it is difficult to control a firm's image (and the extent to which it is deemed to be an attractive employer) globally. A report by The Conference Board on employer branding suggests that while organizations believed that having a strong employer brand was a competitive and strategic advantage, large and diversified global firms found it a challenge to convey a unified, coherent brand image appropriate to different cultures and nationalities.[5] It is also the case that many large and global firms tend to have a national identity that may also change attractiveness outside of their home countries. For example, BMW may be an attractive employer in Germany; Haier may be an employer of choice in China; IBM may be viewed as a great employer to more Americans. These firms compete extensively beyond their national borders, not only for market share, but also for top talent.

6.2.2   Strategic and Global Issues in Selection

As described in Chapter 2, the three strategic possibilities can be applied to developing employee selection practices around the world. Firms have the option to try to have a common set of selection practices, replicating, for example, the parent company's system across all foreign subsidiaries. Another option would be for a firm to design different employee selection systems locally or regionally. A third option would be some hybrid between a local and a global (or centrally controlled) solution, perhaps a common selection system developed with global input or an employee selection system that has a common structure with local adaptation.

The decision regarding the approach to employee selection should also be contingent on the overall orientation for a given firm and for a given role. For example, in firms where there is a strategic need for local responsiveness among sales associates, their selection systems may be different, conforming to local differences on how goods are sold, expectations among clients, behavioral preferences for sales associates nationally, and the like. Consistent with this strategy, decisions are made at the national or subsidiary level regarding the way in which sales associates are selected, the dimensions or competencies on which prospective sales candidates are evaluated, the method to be used in selection, and so forth. Companies operating with an exporter or standardization strategy for the same job title of sales associate will be more likely to maintain a common standard, use common tools, share a common set of interview questions, etc. for selecting sales associates around the world.

For employee selection across the global workforce, regardless of strategic orientation, the first step is to determine the broad content domain for a given position – repeating this step across countries for the same position to determine whether the jobs are, in fact, comparable. In test validity language, the selection systems would need to tap the same performance domain across countries. For example, Asian managers may emphasize cooperation and teamwork when assessing leaders, whereas American managers may emphasize assertiveness and independence for the same leadership position. In this example, the content domain for a given leadership role may not be conceptually equivalent across cultures. In firms operating from local adaptation strategy and transferring people across borders, the conceptual equivalence challenge may be further exacerbated. If a candidate is selected in one country (predicting a country-specific performance domain) and is transferred to another country in the same role where the performance domain may differ (as in the leadership example above), the validity of the original selection system will be lowered[6].

Many global firms have corporate-level cultural competencies which appear in managerial selection systems around the world. These corporate-level managerial competencies may include dimensions such as managing with integrity, taking appropriate risks, being customer-focused, being results-oriented, and the like. After these broad performance dimensions are named, the challenge turns to creating conceptual equivalence for each competence across cultures. For example, what does *managing with integrity* mean behaviorally within the organization – and what does it mean behaviorally within each of the cultures where the firm operates?

The firm needs to be clear on two critical questions in developing these competency-based selection and assessment systems when managing the global workforce:

1 Does the firm want a common set of behaviors that may be culturally inconsistent for some?
2 Or, does the firm want locally consistent behavioral norms for common dimensions that may be inconsistent across cultures?

As you can easily imagine, obtaining agreement on the answers to these two questions can be daunting. When left unanswered, however, managers tend to use local norms and preferences for employee selection and assessment and managing employees' competencies, in general. It takes far longer to gain conceptual equivalence on any given competency. Gaining conceptual equivalence may be easier for more behaviorally objective competencies, such as *operating safely*, and more difficult for more subjective competencies, such as *managing with integrity*. The complexity of global selection systems is further complicated given that developing candidate selection and assessment tools, which are conceptually comparable across cultures, are beyond the mere translation of the words on a selection test, the questions in a pre-employment interview, etc. Let's consider some of the key challenges in developing global employee selection methods:[7]

Creating conceptual equivalence when needed. Cross-national work values can affect the weight that one places on a particular selection dimension or the actual interpretation of the applicants' behaviors, creating a challenge for assessing candidates through a single cultural lens. Conceptual equivalence occurs when constructs have similar meanings across cultures and is necessary for comparisons of candidates to be meaningful. Customer service orientation, for example, may translate into "complete attention to customers' needs" in Japan where anticipating needs is important. In Italy, however, where shopkeepers with exquisite taste are highly valued, customer service may mean "providing honest feedback." In this example, "customer service orientation" lacks conceptual equivalence. However, in both Japan and Italy, the construct "expending effort for clients" may be defined as working hard to find a desired item or to help a client resolve a problem. In this example, "expending effort for clients" does possess conceptual equivalence. Maximizing conceptual equivalence may be especially problematic when constructs in the content domain are more subjective and less objective.

Understanding the appropriateness of selection methods across cultures. Once the dimensions to be included in the selection system have been established, the next cross-cultural concern would be the appropriateness of the assessment method and the logistics of those methods in a given cross-cultural context. With respect to testing methods, some methods are perceived more favorably by applicants around the globe. Applicants across Western cultures perceive job-related interviews, résumés, and work samples more favorably than testing (e.g. personality tests, cognitive ability tests) and reference checking.[8] While applicant reactions to selection methods may be generally similar across countries, their usage is not. Multi-country survey-based studies found that countries did vary significantly in terms of employee selection procedures used, specifically finding that national-level cultural values, such as uncertainty avoidance, predicted what selection procedures were more likely to be used across countries.[9] Countries higher in risk aversion were more likely to rely more heavily on interviews and testing, presumably as a way of reducing hiring risks. Further research in the area of cross-cultural differences in use and acceptance of selection methods is important to further understanding of global employee selection methods and, hopefully, reducing resistance to them (for a review, see Lievens, 2007).[10]

Conducting interviews and making assessments of candidates cross-nationally. Selection is most often conducted through supervisors' interviews of candidates. Interviews are especially challenging when supervisors from one culture are interviewing or assessing candidates from another culture because behaviors may be interpreted through a cultural lens and unintended inferences may be made. For example, eye contact, while very important in many Western cultures as a demonstration of honesty, would be disrespectful and inappropriate in some Asian cultures.

When making more subjective assessments, raters of different national backgrounds may have different standards across competencies. If, from a strategic perspective, organizations would like to maintain common assessment standards globally for more subjective dimensions, then they should consider rater training. *Frame-of-reference training*, as a rater training technique offered to those who will be conducting assessments, could be used. Frame-of-reference training facilitates the ability for diverse raters to make reliable assessments by training on how to interpret behaviors through a common behavioral lens. This type of training has been shown to be highly effective at reducing the idiosyncratic standards of performance raters.[11]

Understanding national differences in HR systems affecting employee selection. As we discussed in Chapter 3, HR systems vary from country to country depending on some relatively fixed dimensions including the given country's work systems. These country-level factors may affect the practice of employee selection across given countries as they affect employment laws, workforce competence, and availability of talent. For example, the United States has a body of laws stemming from the initial fair non-discriminatory employment legislation covered in the Civil Rights Act of 1964, Title VII, the Age Discrimination Act, and the Americans with Disabilities Act. As in the USA, in almost every country laws exist which define the type of firm that must abide by the given law prohibiting discrimination (e.g. size of the firm, public or private sector) and defines who is considered to be protected under the given law (e.g. race, sex, age, sexual orientation). In India, for example, Article 15 of the Indian Constitution prohibits discrimination on the grounds of caste. Many countries around the world have laws which state that selection systems cannot discriminate against protected groups; however, the way in which discrimination is determined and the penalty for violating the law varies greatly from country to country.

Understandably, these challenges in selecting employees across countries within a company's global workforce are complex, nuanced, and very challenging. The benefits to the firm that dedicates the time to answer these strategic questions about employee competencies globally – and, in turn, effectively selects for them within the various countries where it operates – has a competitive advantage within its global workforce for implementing global business strategy.

6.2.3   Strategic and Global Issues in Training and Development

Once individuals are selected into the organization, the next set of tools for managing their competencies is training and development. The terms *training* and *development* tend to be combined to signify the set of activities used by firms to develop the competencies of their employees. The objective of both training and development in firms operating globally is *to foster learning among employees and develop their competencies so they, in turn, can enhance the organization's global competitiveness and effectiveness*. While similar in objective, the goals of training and development are different. In general terms, development has broader organizational focus with a future-oriented time frame, compared to training. Training tends to be individually focused with a present (or near-future) time frame. Training also addresses particular deficiencies in individuals, develops specific competencies, focuses on more tangible aspects of improving performance, and tends to be oriented towards solving short-term performance concerns. Development, on the other hand, is a broader effort which is linked to improving the global organization's competence to fulfill a strategic need in the future.

Determining the content of training. As with employee selection and assessment discussed in the previous section, decisions regarding training and development are also contingent on the same strategic questions about local responsiveness and global integration or consistency. Thus, as with employee selection, depending on strategic needs for any given competency, training and development can be managed locally, regionally, or globally – or within business units. Returning to the Shell safety example for a moment, *operating safely* is a competency that has common behavioral norms and is managed for consistency. Shell's goal is a consistent global norm for safety – zero accidents. For any firm opting for common competencies (with common behavioral indicators), training can be managed centrally with global coordination and then delivered to employees around the world. For all global training decisions, it is important to consider which behaviors should be globally consistent (and trained consistently) and which should be more locally oriented (and trained for local norms).

Local responsive training programs are designed to maximize employee competencies as they perform tasks in a given cultural context. Let's consider the cross-national sales scenario as a typical case where behavioral adaptation is often needed in order to be successful. Let's consider the case of training Indian call center associates on the best way to be successful with their American clients. This is an example of training which is designed specifically for employees within a given country to manage customer service expectations of those from another country. The training, in this situation, is Indian-specific (i.e. the challenges they specifically may have) by instructing Indian associates on the culturally appropriate way to speak with American customers. If the same Indian customer service associates were serving fellow Indian or British clients, in this example, the training would vary. The training programs, in this case, are culturally specific. An extract from a *Wall Street Journal* article on Indian call centers servicing American clients illustrates this type of culturally oriented, locally responsive training.

> In an American-culture training class at Wipro, students identify Indian stereotypes (superstitious, religious and helpful) and American stereotypes (sports-loving, punctual, not as knowledgeable about computers as they think). The point is to identify shallow images as barriers to good communications so they can be overcome. The class reviews cultural differences big and small. As a "high-context" culture where what is communicated is more internalized (say, in a family), Indians can seem to be beating around the bush to Americans, who are part of a low-context culture in which communications need to be more explicit. "If you like to talk and you're dealing with a low-context person," explains the instructor, Roger George, "you might want to keep it simple and get to the point."[12]

Determining the methods for training delivery. In addition to the content included in training, the best way to deliver training programs may also be culturally bound. For example, Herman Aguinis found that the case study method of content delivery is very popular among US trainees (especially when training on business skills). This method, however, is not the most appropriate method of content delivery for Chinese trainees. Chinese participants are more likely not to express their opinions openly, as compared to US trainees, and thus make the training method inappropriate and ineffective in this cultural context. It is useful for training professionals working for global organizations to take into consideration participants' cultural background and values when developing and delivering training programs.[13]

Integrating training and development. Development programs tend to focus on how competencies will be developed and leveraged at the organization and strategic level. Many employee development programs include some training programs, applied to a group of employees in a systematic way. An example of this would be if an information technology organization (with a growing global presence) predicted that most of its programmers would be working in worldwide geographically distributed teams in the next few years – and, in an effort to be proactive, sent all programmers to the following training sessions:

- Multicultural team-building
- Effective remote communication
- How to run a tele-meeting
- Cross-cultural differences in email and phone communication.

In this example training and development are complementary functions. Development may extend beyond training programs to other activities such as stretch assignments, opportunities to be coached or mentored, returning to college for an advanced degree, and the like. As training, these employee development opportunities should be leveraged globally in a way that is consistent with the firm's strategy for managing the global workforce. When training and development programs work effectively around the world to increase employee competencies where needed, within a firm's various subsidiaries, the firm will benefit from a competitive advantage through its global workforce. The next section of this chapter will focus on competency development for global business leaders, a strategic directive for many global firms today as their need for culturally agile, globally competent leaders continues to rise.

6.3 Managing Global Leadership Development: Successfully Developing Global Leaders with Cultural Agility

Around the world, globalization has created a demand for culturally agile global business leaders who can operate successfully across borders and in multicultural situations. Global leaders are not necessarily international assignees (discussed in the subsequent section).

Not all international assignees are global leaders and not all global leaders have had international assignments. Global leaders are executives who are in jobs with some international scope, who must effectively manage through the complex, changing, and often ambiguous global environment. The following 10 tasks or activities are found to be common among those in global leadership positions.[14]

1 Global leaders work with colleagues from other countries.
2 Global leaders interact with external clients from other countries.
3 Global leaders interact with internal clients from other countries.
4 Global leaders will often speak another language (other than their mother tongue) at work.
5 Global leaders supervise employees who are of different nationalities.
6 Global leaders develop a strategic business plan on a worldwide basis.
7 Global leaders manage a budget on a worldwide basis.
8 Global leaders negotiate in other countries or with people from other countries.
9 Global leaders manage foreign suppliers or vendors.
10 Global leaders manage risk on a worldwide basis for your unit.

To successfully complete these 10 tasks, global leaders must learn to be culturally agile as they adapt across multicultural contexts.

As described in Chapter 4, there are three cultural orientations present in those who are culturally agile – cultural minimalism, cultural adaptation, and cultural integration. In the most culturally agile leaders, each of these orientations will be leveraged depending on the contextual situation in which they are operating. There are selection, training, and development practices human resource professionals can use to produce a better pipeline of managers and individual contributors who are culturally agile, who can quickly, comfortably and successfully work in multicultural situations and with people from different cultures.

6.3.1 Selecting Those with Cultural Agility

Some individuals have significant multicultural experiences before starting their professional careers. They may, for example, have lived in a multicultural household or attended school in another country. Some may speak multiple languages. Some may have personality characteristics, such as openness or extraversion, which draw them to intercultural experiences. Collectively, these characteristics may indicate that a given individual will either have cultural agility or be predisposed to readily gaining cultural agility when brought into the organization.

One goal for HR professionals responsible for managing a global workforce, especially those in the area of leadership development, should be to identify people who either have cultural agility or a predisposition for cultural agility. They may do this by interviewing (See Text Box 6.1) or assessing individuals' biodata indicators, such as international education or number of languages spoken. Assessment may also be conducted by self-assessment combined with a facilitated discussion around a tailored development plan. In this case, organizations may use a self-assessment tool such as the Self-Assessment for Global Endeavors for Global Business Leaders (The SAGE for Global Business Leaders), designed for self-awareness, as a guide to illustrate individuals' strengths and potential opportunities for personal and professional development. Regardless of the method used, if the goal is to increase the number of culturally agile leaders in the pipeline, it is important to consider the internationally oriented experiences of those who are entering the organization and, even more important, the presence of characteristics that would predispose individuals to cultural agility from organizationally driven developmental opportunities.

Box 6.1   Sample Cultural Agility Interview Questions

1 Describe a situation where you needed to adapt your leadership behaviors to be effective in an unfamiliar, new or different context (or host culture). What did you do? What were the challenges? How did you manage those challenges?
2 Describe a situation where you needed to maintain your leadership behaviors even though they were counter to preference of those you were leading (or those within the host culture). What did you do? What were the challenges? How did you manage those challenges?
3 Describe a situation where you needed to compromise between your preferences as a leader and those you were leading or those with

whom you were working (or those from the host country). What did you do? What were the challenges? How did you manage those challenges?

4 Describe a cross-national challenge that did not result in the best possible outcome. What happened? What should have happened? What could have been done differently?

5 What characteristics have served you well in unfamiliar (or cross-national) situations?

6.3.2 Training and Developing Cultural Agility

There is a variety of cross-cultural training and developmental opportunities available to improve leaders' cultural knowledge and their performance on global leadership activities – and, in turn, increase their cultural agility. Cross-cultural training and language training are two areas which can be offered to increase individuals' knowledge which, in turn, will be helpful in their development of global leadership competence. As will be described in greater detail in the next section on international assignees, cross-cultural training can help individuals to behave in a more culturally appropriate manner and help managers identify suitable ways of performing their tasks with people from a given culture or in a given country. Speaking another language and living comfortably in another culture are not the goals of global leadership development; they are the mechanisms through which global leadership development can occur and cultural agility can be gained.

Organizations can offer cross-cultural training in a variety of ways, such as online, cultural coaching or small group cross-cultural training. The deepest level of cultural development happens when individuals experience culture for themselves. Experientially, individuals learn from every cross-cultural encounter which includes the following two features:

1 significant peer-to-peer contact with a person or people from a different culture; and

2 an opportunity or opportunities to question one's own assumptions and to realize the cultural limits of one's knowledge base or behaviors.

There are many types of developmental experiences which will offer these features, from participation in global teams to international assignments. However, for these leadership development activities to be effective, they would need both features.

Developmental international assignments, described in the next section, are an example of a high-contact developmental opportunity as they provide an opportunity to live in different countries and develop an extensive understanding of the local culture by interacting with host nationals and participating in local traditions and customs. International assignments increase cultural agility through high-level contact with people from different cultures. Those on international assignments report that they develop an appreciation for new things, become culturally sensitive, and learn to respect values and customs different than their own. The ability for individuals to understand the extent to which their skills and abilities are culturally bound is one of the most powerful lessons learned on international assignments related to global leadership competence.

How do developmental experiences improve global leadership competence and cultural agility? Greater participation in these high-contact cross-cultural leadership development experiences allows individuals to improve their ability to reproduce culturally appropriate skills and behaviors.[15] The more exposure an individual has with high-contact cross-cultural leadership development experiences, the more opportunity he or she has to practice the modeled behavior and to refine the ability to reproduce the modeled behavior at a later time in the appropriate situation. Having a deep understanding of the differences between one's own culture and the culture of another is foundational for cultural agility. When one, in turn, uses their deep cultural understanding appropriately (as a minimalist, adaptor, integrator, depending on the situation), they have gained cultural agility.

6.4 Managing Global Mobility: Successfully Managing the Competencies of International Assignees Who Work Cross-Nationally

One of the most powerful developmental opportunities for helping predisposed individuals gain cultural agility is to have them live and work in another country. Individuals who live and work cross-nationally have been collectively called expatriate or international assignees. International assignees are important for the success of global firms as they are often responsible for tasks such as opening new international markets, handling politically sensitive business, training host national employees; therefore, international assignees who can live comfortably and work effectively are indispensible for firms operating globally – and managing these international assignees to be both comfortable and effective is a pervasive challenge for HR departments in global firms. The three most common reasons international assignees are transferred from one country to another country are:

1 to support *organizational development,* which refers to the coordination and control of international operations through socialization and informal networks;
2 to *fill positions* that cannot be staffed locally because of a lack of technical or managerial skills; and
3 to support *management development* by enabling high potential individuals to acquire international experience.[16]

These three reasons for international assignments are not mutually exclusive and for most firms the first point is inherent in all assignments; international assignments are a mechanism for control and coordination between a given foreign subsidiary and the parent organization. As a means of fostering the parent corporate culture, firms may place international assignees from headquarters (or those who have been with the firm for years) in key leadership positions in host national subsidiaries. From these leadership roles, international assignees are able to enact the parent company's way of doing things.

Most international assignments vary along two dimensions: (1) the extent to which the assignment will require intercultural competence and (2) the extent to which the assignment is intended to be developmental, enhancing skills, for the employee; and fall into three major categories: technical or functional, strategic, and developmental. These two continua form a basic classification system resulting in the following three general categories of global assignments: (1) technical or functional assignments, (2) developmental or high potential assignments, and (3) strategic or executive assignments.[17] Technical and functional assignees generally are the most common global assignees in a typical transnational organization and represent almost all functional areas within the organization. Functional assignees are placed in international assignments whenever a technical expertise may be lacking in the host country and they are needed to fill a skill gap. For example, these individuals may be technical experts who are members of implementation teams, operations managers who are overseeing manufacturing facilities, or quality engineers managing supply chains. Given that they are primarily sent to fill a technical need, their professional development is not the intended primary goal for the assignment.

With respect to developmental or high potential assignments, firms are sending employees to another country to develop global competencies as a part of the respective employee's overall career development plan, usually in the context of leadership development. These programs are often rotational – with one of the rotations being in another country. While on this type of assignment, the worker's goal is to develop professional, technical, and intercultural competencies. These rotational assignments, often part of a global leadership development program, include a very structured series of developmental experiences, such as moving across functional areas, product lines, business units, and geographical regions. Strategic or executive assignments are usually filled by senior leaders (directors, vice presidents, general managers) who are being developed for progressively higher-level executive positions. They are also sent to fill specific needs in the organization, which may be entering new markets, managing joint ventures, running a function within a foreign subsidiary, and the like. These individuals often need a high level of intercultural sensitivity in order to be successful on their global assignments.

In technical assignments there are no stated employee developmental components. These assignments require few, if any, intercultural skills to be successfully completed. Technical assignees are sent internationally solely to complete the job and return home. *Functional* assignees are sent to complete a job and return home, and employee development is not a stated organizational goal. To be successful, however, functional assignees must be interculturally competent. While abroad, functional assignees may develop new skills (although not an intended assignment goal). Sales and marketing staff, production managers, and contract negotiators often fall into this category.

6.4.1   Self-Assessment and Decision-Making

Long before assignments are available, key employees should consider the viability of a future global assignment. International assignments are not right for every person or every family (See Text Box 6.2). Full involvement throughout the process by the employee and all accompanying family members is critical. To further aid in the decision making process, self-selection tools are useful when employees are contemplating pursuit of a global assignment. At this early stage, employees and their families are able to critically evaluate themselves on key issues before making the decision to accept an international assignment. Research has shown that self-selection tools help employees make a thoroughly informed and realistic decision before putting their names forward as candidates for global assignments – ultimately leading to greater international assignee success. Those candidates who have some interest in an international assignment should nominate themselves for inclusion in the "potential expatriate" database. Information on prospective individuals should indicate where they are willing to relocate, when they are available, what languages they speak, whether they have any experience that is relevant to an international assignment, and so forth.

Box 6.2   International Assignee Candidate's Decision-Making Checklist

The Top 10 Questions to Consider Before You Relocate
- ✓ Do you have all the information you need to make an informed decision for you and your family – and have you thought through the personal implications of this move for you and your family members?
- ✓ Are your family members willing to relocate (even happy about the opportunity)?
- ✓ Is your marriage/family stable and cohesive? Communicative? Adaptable?
- ✓ Is your spouse employed – and, if so, have you discussed the implications this will have on his or her career?
- ✓ Do you know what type of social, instrumental, and information-based support is available for you and your family during the assignment?

✓ Do you have the characteristics that will help you on the assignment – emotional strength, openness, flexibility, extraversion, intellectual curiosity, and autonomy?
✓ Is there clarity around what you are being asked to do and what competencies you are expected to gain or develop?
✓ Do you know what type of professional support is available for you during the assignment?
✓ Do you know how you will be evaluated?
✓ Are you happy about this opportunity?

Self-assessment also gives expatriate candidates an opportunity to consider their family situation and whether the assignment would be the best thing for the expatriate candidate's family members. Spouses, for example, may not be able to work given a host country's visa limitations. Children may have special needs for medical or educational assistance. In addition, a family's characteristics as a unit (e.g. their cohesion, communication, and adaptability) will spill over and ultimately influence the adjustment and performance of the international assignee. Figure 6.1 shows how a family's attributes can influence the outcome of the international assignment. It should

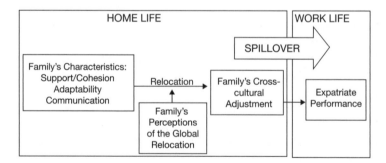

Figure 6.1   Family-level Characteristics and Adjustment Can Influence the Outcome of the International Assignment
Source: Caligiuri, P. M., Hyland, M., and Joshi, A., "Families on global assignments: Applying work/family theories abroad". Chapter in A. Rahim (ed.), *Current Topics in Management*, Vol. 3 (Greenwich, CT: JAI Press, 1998), pp. 313–328.

not be surprising that many research studies have identified a positive influence of the adjustment of an accompanying spouse or partner and child or children on the expatriate. Due to their influence on expatriate adjustment, and ultimately performance, spouses and children need to be included in the selection process in a way that preserves the family's privacy.

6.4.2 Selection and Assessment

Considering that international assignments are job contexts, not job descriptions, the predictors of international assignee success relate more to the idea of living and working in a foreign country as opposed to successfully completing any specific job-related tasks. There are a variety of individual-level antecedents of international assignee success discussed in this section including personality characteristics, language skills, and prior experience of living in a different country.

Personality characteristics should be assessed when deciding who to send on international assignments. Researchers have found that successful and well-adjusted international assignees tend to share certain personality traits enabling them to be open and receptive to learning the norms of new cultures, to initiate contact with host nationals, to gather cultural information, and to handle the higher amounts of stress associated with the ambiguity of their new environments – all important for international assignee success. Based on personality theory, the most important dispositional factors to include in assessments are:

1 Extraversion – It is important to help international assignees learn the work and nonwork social culture in the host country related to international assignee success.
2 Agreeableness – The ability to form reciprocal social alliances and build relationships in the host country are achieved through this personality characteristic.
3 Conscientiousness – Trusted and conscientious employees are more likely to become leaders, gain status, get promoted, earn higher salaries, etc. The tenacity of conscientious employees is often needed in international assignments.

4 Emotional Stability – Given that stress is often associated with living and working in an ambiguous and unfamiliar environment, emotional stability is an important personality characteristic for international assignees' success in the host country.
5 Openness or Intellect – Openness is related to international assignee success because individuals higher in this personality characteristic will have fewer rigid views of right and wrong, appropriate and inappropriate, etc. They are more likely to be accepting of the new culture.

Collectively, these personality characteristics could be included in a valid selection system for prospective international assignees. However, the absolute level of each personality characteristic would be contingent upon the type of international assignment under consideration.

Like personality characteristics, language skills and prior international experience may be included in a selection system – but may not be critical (or even relevant), depending on the type of assignment. Certainly, having language skills will help international assignees adjust to their host country because speaking the host national language would help them integrate into the culture faster than someone without the language skills.

Prior experience in the host culture is also useful; having experience in that culture suggests that the prospective international assignee knows what he or she is to expect in the host country. More formally, some firms encourage international assignees to visit the host country to interview, understand the requirements of the assignment, or meet with colleagues who have worked in the host country in the decision making or selection phases. These practices help create a realistic preview among international assignee candidates as they help them create realistic expectations during (or prior to) selection.

With the diversity of roles among international assignees, different international assignees will likely require different levels of relevant attributes (e.g. language fluency, openness, and technical skills). As such, a single "international assignment selection system" that will be valid across all types of assignees is not often possible. However, once the requirements of a given international assignment have been determined, many possibilities exist to assess the candidates on job-related dimensions. For example, greater emphasis would be placed on personality characteristics (such as sociability and openness) when assessing a candidate for a developmental or strategic assignment – requiring much more host national contact, compared to a more technical international assignment. In the best case, a thorough assessment can be conducted through a variety of valid formal selection methods: paper and pencil tests, assessment centers, interviews, behavioral observations, and the like.

6.4.3   *Cross-Cultural Training*

In addition to comprehensive self-selection and selection programs, success in international assignments may be facilitated through cross-cultural training and language training. By definition, cross-cultural training can help individuals behave in a more culturally appropriate manner and help managers identify suitable ways of performing their tasks with people from a given culture or in a given country. Cross-cultural training may also help individuals develop methods for coping with the uncertainty when working with people from different cultures or in foreign countries and may help them form realistic expectations for their cross-national interactions and experiences. The most basic cross-cultural training is a pre-departure cross-cultural orientation. The immediate goal of cross-cultural orientation is to help an international assignee learn the basics (e.g. currency, public transportation, working hours) to comfortably live and work in the host country.

Increasing in popularity, there are various online cross-cultural training tools available to help individuals to self-assess and gain cultural knowledge. RW-3's Culture Wizard is one such web-based tool that helps in providing valuable insight on ways to successfully work with people and teams from different cultures. RW-3's tools are standalone, self-guided learning experiences that are designed to create an awareness of the importance of culture in everyday business interaction and illustrate the impact that culture has on people's values, beliefs, and behaviors. Figure 6.2 offers an example of this online cross-cultural training tool. The online facility allows learners to assess their needs, evaluate their life experiences and develop programs that are tailored to their individual information requirements. For example, the tools range from assessments for global business professionals and international assignees to a full cross-cultural

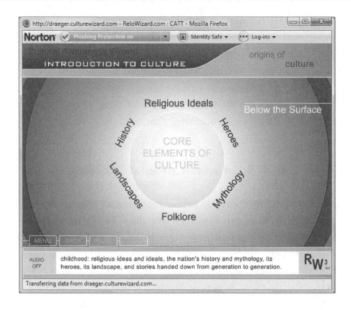

Figure 6.2

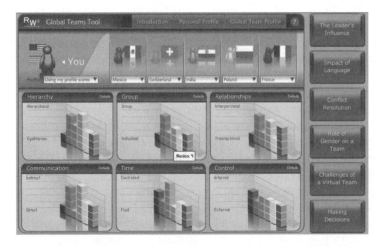

Figure 6.2 Example of an Online Team-oriented Cross-cultural Training Program from RW-3.

course and business applications such as managing global teams and collaborating across styles and cultures. Text Box 6.3 offers questions to consider when evaluating online cross-cultural training.

Box 6.3 Evaluating Electronic-based Cross-Cultural Training

With the inception of e-learning in many organizations, cross-cultural training programs are also beginning to be delivered via the Internet or through organizations' intranet systems. To evaluate these electronic delivery CCT programs, one should determine to what extent this system provides a complete program of CCT, covering everything that would normally be covered in a comprehensive cross-cultural training program. You can evaluate the content of e-CCT by asking these questions:

• Does the program have a section explaining what culture is and how it affects daily life? Evaluate how well these are explained.
• Does the program provide a framework (or model) for understanding culture - including several dimensions of culture? Are they easy to understand and apply to real life?

- Does the program allow the participant an opportunity to evaluate his or her own cultural values? Is the cultural value assessment a reliable instrument? Ask to see the reliability evidence for the scales measuring the various dimensions (e.g., alpha coefficients).
- Can the participant's cultural values be evaluated against the host country's cultural values? How were the values applied to the host countries validated (be careful that they were not created by the author's perceptions)? Ask to see a report on the development process and the validation studies.
- Does the program effectively explain the challenges of culture shock? Evaluate how well this concept is described.
- Does the program include a self-assessment to help the expatriate consider the challenges for his or her family, career, and personality? As before, check carefully the reliability of the scales used to assess these concepts and validity reports which document the linkage between the dimensions assessed and criteria of expatriate success. (Be careful because there are tools that have been written to "look" relevant – which have no practical or substantiated worth.)

In addition to the content of the system, several other factors should be considered when evaluating an electronic-delivery cross-cultural training program. Some other factors to evaluate include:

- Is the program self-directed? Is the participant able to move in and out of the program easily? Are the basic materials presented before the more challenging information is offered? Would they need to start over if they exit the program?
- Can expatriates access this information in real time, while they are on assignment? Are they allowed free access to the site – or do they have limited time or a limited number of accesses to the site?
- Is the system designed to tailor the information for the expatriates as they work through the training program? For example, does the system remember the country in which the expatriate is living, that she has two children, etc.? The more tailoring provided by the system, the more receptive the expatriate will be to interacting with the e-CCT system.
- Is the system relatively easy to use? Does it load quickly? Is the system easy to navigate?

- Is the information current? Check the country information – especially with those also offering broader relocation provisions (home searches, schools, etc.).

While e-CCT may be a cost-effective way to deliver training to many expatriates, international HR professionals are advised to select their vendors carefully – not solely on low cost or flashy graphics.

Source:
Tarique, I. and Caligiuri, P. M., Training and development of international staff. Invited chapter in Harzing and Van Ruysseveldt (Eds.), *International Human Resource Management* (Sage Publications, 2004).

Like cultural training, language training is also useful in improving the language skills necessary for communication in a given host country's language. Language training aids in communications, demonstrates an attitude of attempting to learn about the host culture, enables one to be polite, permits understanding not otherwise available and is an intrinsic part of the culture. Like cultural training, language training can be gained more informally through self-directed audio courses or formally in a classroom setting or in formal immersion programs.

Another outstanding practice is the offering of sequential cross-cultural training once international assignees are in their host country. It is then when they start to experience the cross-national differences described in Chapter 4. The cross-cultural coaches who work with international assignees are able to intervene and explain cultural norms, help international assignees build cultural awareness, work on cultural "blind-spots", and help develop competencies for becoming effective in an international environment. Occasionally, cross-national coaches are assigned for a specific task (e.g. delivering an important speech in another country, negotiating an international joint venture).

6.4.4 *Work–Life Balance and Support Practices*

International assignments permeate both work life (e.g. new job, new colleagues, new organizational norms) and home life (e.g. new house, new friends, new city). Therefore, achieving work–life balance while on international assignments can be especially difficult. During international assignments, the boundaries between organizational support and personal privacy are increasingly blurred. Most organizations pragmatically understand that in order to manage the risk of a potentially unsuccessful global assignment, they must help their international assignees manage nonwork factors, such as establishing social ties, finding social communities, re-establishing hobbies, sports, places of worship, and the like in the host countries.

In most cases, international assignees' lives are embedded into those of their partners, children, friends, and other loved ones. Partners and children, who often accompany them to the host country, have their lives disrupted for the sake of the assignees' job. Their experiences can often have a profound influence on the assignees' sense of work–life balance and, subsequently, on the outcome of international assignments. Many progressive firms have also recognized the powerful influence that accompanying partners and children have on the work–life balance of their international assignees, and in turn, their job performance. As such, these organizations become more involved in the nonwork aspects of their assignees and families. Treading carefully to preserve individual privacy, organizations (to varying degrees) have developed programs, policies, and practices designed for international assignees and their family members to help improve their work–life balance. Some examples of the support practices organizations have developed to encourage international assignees' work–life balance include cross-cultural training for families, in-country support, career assistance, accompanying partner support, and general work–life assistance.

Even though spouses and accompanying partners voluntarily choose to place their careers on the backburner, losing one's job is still a stressful experience. Accompanying partners not only lose their income, but also lose another source of social and professional identity; this loss compounds the feeling of low self-esteem, social isolation, and anxiety normally experienced during international transitions. In 2002, the Global Relocations Trends survey found that 56 % of the companies made provisions for accompanying partners' careers: 36 % offered education or training assistance, 31 % offered career enhancement reimbursement, 28 % offered career planning assistance, and 21% offered assistance finding employment.

There are other tangible services that companies offer accompanying partners on global assignments. These include: monetary policies such as paying fees required by employment agencies in the host countries, offering seed money to start a new business, paying fees to join professional associations, compensation of the accompanying partner's lost wages and benefits, or offering financial support to engage in volunteer service. Other tangible services companies offer are nonmonetary but are also considered extremely useful for accompanying partners. These include: organization-sponsored support groups for partners, employment networks coordinated with other global firms, and office space in the host location for the purpose of job hunting.

In addition to spouses or accompanying partners, the children of expatriates may also experience problems in adjustment. Uprooting a child from a place that is an important identity source can be a stressful experience. In addition to concerns over availability of high quality education, one also needs to consider the emotional stress children undergo during periods of transition. Children can face obstacles such as saying goodbye to friends, making new friends, starting a new school, communicating through language barriers, having inadequate peer relations, lacking in peer acceptance (especially problematic for teenagers), and overall disruption to personal life. If not adequately supported by the parents, children may feel lonely and isolated, uncertain about their identity, and experience diminished self-esteem. The transition poses extraordinary demands on children of all ages, and it is critical that parents acknowledge this and do their best to help children through this adjustment phase.

6.4.5 Repatriation

Repatriates, who have completed an international assignment, can help establish and expand firms' collective international business acumen because, when successful, they possess first-hand knowledge of particular cultural contexts, including information about specific markets and customers. If assignments go well, repatriates understand how the company is perceived in another country; they are part of a global social network that can advance the company's business around the world and can accelerate the transfer of knowledge from host countries to headquarters, and vice versa. For these reasons, many companies view their successful repatriates as an important human capital investment. Despite the strategic and financial importance of repatriates, there is evidence that many firms fail to capitalize on these human investments, because many of their assignees leave the company after the assignment is completed.

The loss of an internationally proficient repatriate may indirectly translate into providing advantage to direct competitors, as repatriates are likely to find jobs with competitors, thus providing the competitors with valuable human assets. In addition, high turnover among repatriates compromises the company's ability to recruit future expatriates because it signals to other employees in the company that, despite the stated message to the contrary, international assignments may have a negative impact on one's career. Given this strategic human capital issue, ways to increase repatriate retention and lower their turnover are an important consideration for those in HR roles.

Various factors affect whether expatriates remain with their company upon repatriation, which include: being placed in non-challenging jobs, lack of promotion opportunities, loss of status and autonomy, lack of career planning and counseling, lack of support on behalf of managers and colleagues, and sluggish career advancement. Of these many factors, it is not surprising that the most important one is the repatriates' perception of how well the MNCs managed their repatriation process. This suggests that if the potential repatriation problems are appropriately addressed by the firm in advance, repatriate turnover will occur less often. Thus, the repatriates who perceive that they have more support from their organization will be more committed to that organization – and will be more likely to stay with it after repatriation.

Adapted from previous work by Paula Caligiuri and Mila Lazarova, proactive recommendations for strategic repatriation are listed below. These practices are especially important for those assignees in strategic or developmental roles where their global experiences (and, hopefully, developed competencies) are needed in the organization after the completion of the assignment. They include the following:[18]

1   Career planning is a critical function for retaining international assignees upon repatriation. Between six and 12 months before the end of the global assignment, global firms should offer multiple re-entry sessions or career planning sessions to discuss the international assignee's concerns regarding repatriation; for example, career objectives and performance. The intention of

these career planning re-entry sessions is to give the international assignee a sense of security regarding his or her future with the company.

2 To reduce ambiguity about the international assignee's future, offer a written guarantee or repatriation agreement. This repatriation agreement outlines the type of position the international assignee will be placed in upon return from global assignment.

3 One popular practice used in proactive repatriation systems is mentoring. Mentors keep the international assignee abreast of important occurrences while he or she is on global assignment and help the international assignee stay connected with the organization. A mentor also guides the international assignee's future career with the organization by being the international assignee's internal champion.

4 Organizations should offer a reorientation program to brief returning international assignees on the changes in the company, such as in policies, personnel, and strategy. This should be provided immediately upon return from the assignment, when the repatriate returns to work.

5 Repatriation training seminars should be offered to employees and their families. These repatriation training seminars will address international assignees' emotional concerns upon returning home. This repatriation training should improve re-entry adjustment.

6 Another recommendation is financial counseling and financial or tax assistance. This counseling helps repatriates adjust back to their lifestyles without the additional allowances of the international assignee position.

7 Lifestyle counseling is also beneficial to employees and their families, as their lifestyles are likely to change dramatically when they return to their home countries.

8 Global firms can also offer a repatriation adjustment period for the employees to reintegrate without added pressure from the organization. Given the pressures of repatriation both at home and at work, some organizations will reduce the repatriates' travel time, give more vacation time, and so forth.

9 While the international assignee is still on assignment, Global firms should offer opportunities for communication with their home office. For example, the international assignee could be

offered extended home visits during which he or she is expected to be visible at the office. Another possibility is to encourage communication with colleagues and mentors back home to maintain his or her network, and so on.

10 Organizations should show visible signs that they value the international experience (e.g. promoting the repatriate upon return, maintaining position prestige and status, or additional compensation for completing the assignment). This will create the perception within the organization that global experience is beneficial for one's career. This will also help produce a culture in which global experience should not be disregarded.

Repatriation tends to play out very differently depending on the category of global assignment. For example, technical assignees are generally in high demand around the organization – and their next position is often known well in advance of the end of the assignment. The strategic and developmental assignees generally have very thorough developmental plans. Thus, career planning and repatriation is usually less of a challenge for this group. The functional assignees, those generally sent to fill a technical need in a host country without necessarily being sent to develop intercultural competence, tend to have the greatest difficulty being reabsorbed into the home country location; as their role was primarily to fill a technical need, their newly developed competence is not needed in the next position. It is important to understand the unique repatriation needs for each category of global assignee to more strategically develop an effective repatriation program.

Let's consider three repatriation scenarios, all very plausible, all coexisting within the same firm, and all with different repatriation needs. In the first scenario a firm identifies developmental goals for some of its global assignees, the developmental goals are met, and the firm desires to retain the repatriates (and their human capital investment) upon repatriation. In the second scenario the firm sends some highly technical or functional employees on global assignments to accomplish a given task. These assignees do not have any expected developmental goals, but may have gained global competencies during the course of the assignment. Given that the firm may not immediately need their newly developed global competencies, they may risk losing this talent to other firms (possibly competitors) that will value and leverage their newly developed global competencies. In the third scenario, much like the second, the assignees do not have any expected developmental goals and they are sent on a global assignment to fill a technical or functional need. Their skills, however, are not needed by the firm, today or in the foreseeable future (and losing them to a competitor is not a risk). In this case, the skills of the global assignees may not be needed by the firm once the assignment is completed. Repatriation in this case is really the renewal (or termination) of a contract.

A truly strategic repatriation policy will need to consider all three cases, (1) the expatriates who will need to be successfully repatriated in order to competitively leverage their newly developed global competencies, (2) the expatriates who are needed, but may have newly developed competencies that cannot be readily utilized, and (3) the expatriates who completed a contractual agreement and whose skills are no longer needed.

6.5 Chapter Conclusions

The knowledge of organizational strategy – and how managing competencies aligns with your firm's strategy – is critical for managing the global workforce. Two critical areas where selection, training, and development are most important for the functioning of the global firm are in the contexts of developing global leaders with cultural agility and managing international assignments. Whether host national employees, global leaders, or international assignees, human resource professionals and managers in global firms need to remember the following points.

1 **Vary your recruitment message cross-nationally.** It is important to attract the best possible candidates (especially for key roles) from different countries around the world. This may mean flexing your recruitment message from country to country to be most consistent with cultural norms.

2 **Decide when common behaviors (for any given competency) around the world are desired or when local variation on the behavioral indices of competencies is preferred.** Use these strategic decisions to guide the way specific candidate selection systems and employee training and development programs are both designed and implemented.

3 Do not underestimate the difficulty involved in the decisions around #2, or the challenges involved in designing and implementing selection and training programs that follow from these decisions. If behavioral consistency is preferred for any given competency, think through the issues involved in creating conceptually equivalent employee selection systems and training programs for the desired outcome.

4 **Develop culturally agile leaders.** There are two key factors for developing culturally agile leaders: (1) who is in the pipeline from the perspective of their predisposing characteristics and early-life experiences and (2) the type of developmental opportunities they are given (e.g. peer-to-peer contact with colleagues from diverse cultures and opportunities to see the limits of one's knowledge and question one's assumptions).

5 **Manage international assignees using practices including self-selection, candidate assessment, and cross-cultural training.** International assignees, especially those in more developmental and strategic roles, should be selected for their affiliation-oriented personality characteristics and language skills. International assignees, especially those needing to communicate with host nationals, will need language and cultural training.

6 **Support international assignees and their family members.** Remember that an international assignment uproots an entire family, not just the person working for the firm. Family issues are critical in that they will affect the adjustment and performance of international assignees.

7 **Retain repatriates.** Leverage proactive HR practices which can be implemented to try to retain repatriates after their international assignments. Repatriates may have gained critical cultural agility, especially if their assignment involved peer-to-peer interaction with host nationals and significant opportunities to see the limits of their knowledge and question their assumptions.

Notes

1 From Shell's Australian website http://www.shell.com.au/swoceania.
2 From an article on Graham Robinson's Keynote for the IADC Drilling HSE Europe Conference and Exhibition in Amsterdam in 2008, http://drillingcontractor.org.

3 Press Release from Shell Oil, Shell Indonesia Launches "Safety Days 2007" (English) 05/06/2007.

4 Harzing, A. W. (2004). Ideal Jobs and International Student Mobility in the Enlarged European Union. *European Management Journal* 22: 693–703.

5 The Conference Board (2001). *Engaging Employees through Your Brand*. New York: The Conference Board.

6 Lievens, F., "Research on selection in an international context: Current status and future directions" in M. M. Harris (ed.), *Handbook of Research in International Human Resource Management* (Lawrence Erlbaum's Organizations and Management Series, 2007), pp. 107–123

7 Caligiuri, P. and Paul, K. B., "Selection in multinational organizations" (Chapter 34). Refereed book chapter in James L. Farr and Nancy T. Tippins (eds.), *Handbook of Employee Selection* (Lawrence Erlbaum Associates, Inc. Publishers, 2009).

8 Steiner, D. D. and Gilliland, S. W. (2001). Procedural justice in personnel selection: International and cross-cultural perspectives. *International Journal of Selection and Assessment* 9: 124–137.

9 Ryan, A. M., McFarland, L., Baron, H., and Page, R. (1999). An international look at selection practices: Nation and Culture as Explanations for variability in practice. *Personnel Psychology* 52: 359–391.

10 Lievens, F., n. 6 above.

11 Day, D. V. and Sulsky, L. M. (1995). Effects of frame-of-reference training and information configuration on memory organization and rating accuracy. *Journal of Applied Psychology* 80: 158–167.

12 Sandberg, J., "It Says Press Any Key. Where's the Any Key?" India's Call-Center Workers Get Pounded, Pampered, *The Wall Street Journal*, February 20, 2007.

13 Aguinis, H. (2002). *Cross-cultural Implications for Instructional Design, Delivery, and Evaluation*. Panel discussion. Annual Conference of the Society of Industrial and Organizational Psychology, Toronto, Canada.

14 Caligiuri, P. M. (2006). Developing global leaders. *Human Resource Management Review* 16: 219–228.

15 Caligiuri, P. & Tarique, I. (2009). Predicting effectiveness in global leadership activities. *Journal of World Business*, 44, 336–346.

16 Edström, A. and Galbraith J. R. (1977). Transfer of managers as a coordination and control strategy in multinational organizations. *Administrative Science Quarterly* 22(2): 248–263.

17 Caligiuri, P. and Lazarova, M., "Strategic repatriation policies to enhance global leadership development." Invited book chapter for M. Mendenhall, T. Kuehlmann, and G. Stahl (eds), *Developing Global Business Leaders: Policies, Processes, and Innovations* (Quorum Books, 2001), pp. 243–256.

18 Ibid.

CHAPTER 7

Managing Attitudes and Behavior

Motivating and Rewarding the Global Workforce

7.1 Kentucky Fried Chicken Japan: An Illustrative Example

KFC Corporation, headquartered in Louisville, Kentucky, is one of the most successful fast-food chains in the world. In 2009 it had more than 11 000 restaurants in more than 80 countries and territories all over the world. The chain is especially popular in Japan, where it has more than 1100 restaurants around the country. The beginnings of KFC's operations in Japan in the 1970s, however, were not easy. Loy Weston, a former IBM sales representative, was the person in charge of opening the Japanese branch.[1] The KFC home office supplied Weston with a budget, a two-week training course in one of the chain's stores, and an annual salary. Realizing that his assignment required a great deal of freedom and autonomy, they avoided imposing systems of control on him that would have curtailed his initiative. The only requirement given to him was that the restaurants he opened in Japan needed to operate successfully.

Weston, a natural entrepreneur with a great love of Japanese culture, accepted the challenge without hesitation. He knew that he could not turn down a position with these characteristics. The operation, however, quickly developed problems. The budget ran out more quickly than predicted, the work days were exhausting, and the concept of fast food was very difficult to introduce in the

Japanese market in those days. After little more than one year, Weston was obliged to ask the home office for more funds. To his surprise, they agreed readily, thanks to a change in management which approached internationalization as an excellent opportunity for the chain to increase its revenues. It was then that Weston had an inspiration that helped him to turn the situation around. He began to think of KFC-Japan not as a fast-food company but as an industrial enterprise on this model: "Recognizing that we are selling to young, trendy Japanese who wanted to emulate American habits helped us develop a totally new strategic vision."[2]

This new strategic vision led him to choose several locations, and to design several stores and food products, that were quite different from those specified in the KFC operations manual. The pricing policy and the advertising campaign were also markedly different from what existed at headquarters or in other countries. Weston took pride in declaring that all of these decisions were implemented locally without consultation with the home office.

Headquarters, however, was not entirely pleased. They valued highly the importance of maintaining the consistency and reliability of the chain's product line in all of its markets. The adaptations carried out in Japan compromised the chain's image. This led the home office to introduce changes in management with the goal of limiting the autonomy of foreign subsidiaries and assuring that their implementation would be in line with the company's international strategy.

If we think back over the discussion of global business strategy in Chapter 2, the case of KFC-Japan raises many interesting themes. For example, does it make sense to avoid imposing restrictions upon or controlling the actions of foreign subsidiaries' country managers in the implementation (startup) phase? Or, should control come in later when the subsidiaries are more mature? How can we avoid, or manage, goal incongruence between a subsidiary and the parent company? And if (as in this case) the country manager is an expatriate, what can motivate him or her to accept an international assignment and, once in the assignment, what can motivate him or her to expend the effort to carry out his work successfully?

This chapter is dedicated to examining these kinds of questions. We will begin by analyzing the principal tools for guiding attitudes and behavior of local nationals within diverse subsidiaries. Then, as we did in Chapter 6, we will focus the second half of the chapter on managing international assignees. In particular, in the second half of this chapter we will analyze the role played by compensation, by performance evaluations, by the job itself, and by professional career prospects in the motivation of international assignees.

7.2 Managing Attitudes and Behavior in Subsidiaries

Motivating employees to have certain attitudes and display certain behaviors is a challenge for managers, irrespective of culture. People have their own values and attitudes toward work and, therefore, will find different aspects of work or their occupations motivating. Some employees might be motivated by the promise of more free time, others by financial rewards, and others by opportunities to work on plum assignments.

Motivating attitudes and behaviors can be especially challenging across a multinational company given that national-level cultural values are less likely to be shared. While it may be challenging, effectively motivating employees around the world is important because motivated employees are more likely to expend effort, remain committed to their work, and feel more engaged with the company. In multinational companies, to be effective, incentive and reward systems as well as the evaluation systems must effectively align behaviors to business strategy and also align with the preferences in each of the local cultures.

7.2.1 Motivating the Local Workforce

One option to respond to this challenge of motivating employees cross-nationally is to start with an existing headquarters-based HR practice (designed to motivate employee attitudes and behaviors) and attempt to impose it around the world. Unless employees were selected to share common work-related values (e.g. Accenture and McKinsey) in the first place, this exporter approach may have a lower chance of being successful. As you may recall from Chapter 4, there are cultural differences in work values such as how people from different cultures value work. While North Americans typically value work in that they "live to work", Latin-Americans are often said to "work to live". Without pre-selecting individuals who share common (and probably counter-culture) values, the effectiveness of a given HR practice intended to be motivating may depend on how well it matches a national culture's value system.

In many circumstances, if a given value from a national culture and the HR practice designed to motivate employees are congruent (i.e. if employees are asked to behave in a way that is consistent with their own values), employees' expectations will be better met and, as a result, that motivation practice may work well in the subsidiary. The opposite is also true. Given that culture is viewed by its members as the correct way to perceive, think, and feel, when motivation practices and national culture are inconsistent, employees are likely to feel dissatisfied and uncommitted. As a result, they may be less able or willing to perform well.

This problem is magnified when we look for "best practices" on a global level. For example, some of the typical "best American motivation practices" have encountered problems when transferred to certain national settings. Notable failed attempts include efforts to use "Management by Objectives" in France,[3] "individual incentive plans" in Denmark,[4] "participative" management techniques in Russia,[5] "performance appraisal" systems in Hungary,[6] and "open-door" style management in Italy.[7] Without going into all the details for their failures, these examples highlight the fact that there is no one best way of motivating employees across cultures; cultural differences, as discussed in Chapter 4, should be taken carefully into account when it comes to considering how to motivate employees in different cultural settings, especially in companies where there is not a strong and shared corporate culture.

Another approach is to integrate headquarters' HR practices designed to motivate employees with the local approach or adapt HR practices to the values and expectations of local employees. One can easily think about a set of HR practices designed to motivate attitudes and behaviors as a two-phase approach. In the first phase, you can create global motivation initiatives that seek to achieve a minimum set of attitudes and behaviors applicable to all employees. These may be based on a strong and commonly shared set of organizational values. In fact, some companies invest tremendously in this phase to find company-wide common values. Nokia's approach to global employee engagement is an example of this, capturing from their youthful and interconnected employees a shared set of values across Nokia associates. In 2007 Nokia involved more than 2500 employees from around the world in 16 regional events to help find the core Nokia values. There were also online discussion groups and contests to uncover these shared values. From the Nokia website:[8]

> In May 2007, around 13 000 employees registered in the Nokia Way Jam, a 72-hour online discussion to decide on our values and debate our future business strategy. Our business is increasingly focused on the internet and we want the new values to support a more web-based work culture. The collaborative nature of the Jam was itself an expression of Nokia's culture and the value we place on achieving together. Around 77 000 comments were posted during the event.
>
> We analyzed the results of the Jam and identified several key corporate initiatives to be included in our future plans and several initiatives within our business groups. The Jam has prompted new activity and changed some of our business priorities.
>
> In 2007, we invited employees to enter photos in a competition designed to demonstrate our values in action and get people thinking about them. Around 1 700 photos were submitted and 7 700 people voted for their favorites. A selection of pictures will be used to communicate the values around the business.

Clearly, common HR practices designed to incent and engage employees would work well in Nokia locations around the world because a set of core values were determined collaboratively.

As many companies do not have such clearly embedded shared values around the world as Nokia, multinationals may be best advised to consider phase 2, adapting their HR practices designed to incent and engage employees to the host country cultural environment. Let's consider, for example, the idea of employee suggestion systems. Suggestion systems are a motivation tool which consists of training and encouraging employees to submit ideas on how to improve production processes in order to achieve higher quality levels and to reduce production costs. When these ideas have been evaluated and approved by committees set up for this purpose, the ideas are implemented and a percentage of the resulting revenues or savings is transferred to those individuals that submitted them. The practice of the suggestion system is a phase 1 approach. In phase 2, a multinational can allow different applications of this suggestion system within its foreign subsidiaries, allowing cultural preferences to guide the implementation. For example, collectivistic cultures may prefer their suggestions (and subsequent rewards) to be submitted as ideas of the team or work group. Whereas, in strongly individualist cultures such as the United States and Canada, individual employees should be allowed to submit suggestions on their own, and win any subsequent rewards for themselves.

In addition to examining how culture and other contextual factors (e.g. legislation, economic situation, business strategy) may affect motivation of host country nationals, it is also very important to pay particular attention to the way you motivate those who will be in charge of the local operation: the country managers, as they hold a great deal of influence over the management and functioning of the entire subsidiary. This will be discussed in the next section of this chapter.

7.2.2   Motivating Country Managers

Given the broad reach of geographically dispersed multinational companies, many firms find that they need to delegate local decision making to their country manager (i.e. the individual responsible for the successful functioning of a given foreign subsidiary). Both geographic dispersion and multiculturalism make it almost impossible for centralized decision making on all business decisions affecting foreign subsidiaries. KFC, for example, had allowed Loy Weston, their country manager in Japan, to make decisions affecting the startup of the Japanese subsidiary.

Country managers are in a good position for decision making in their respective subsidiaries because they have the knowledge and information about the local market. Presumably, country managers would have the best insight on decisions such as which employees to hire, which commercial strategy to implement, where to locate stores and offices, and the like. If a country manager is not given this level of decision making responsibility, it would be very difficult to respond rapidly to changes in the subsidiary country and adapt to local characteristics, one of the basic capabilities which multinationals need to possess.

Decentralized decision making processes do not only have the advantage of flexibility and local adaptation when needed, they also create a "small business environment" that stimulates entrepreneurship among country managers. Even in large multinationals, country managers can run their operations in many companies like entrepreneurs. Across country managers, many are attracted to this self-governed and results-oriented work environment. This, in fact, becomes a motivating draw for many country managers who relocate from headquarters to work in a foreign subsidiary.[9] Giving country managers more autonomy in their decision making will also serve to generate a greater diversity of ideas and innovation. Ultimately, when the entrepreneurial spirit of country managers is embedded in a knowledge sharing system across subsidiaries, multinationals can benefit from innovation around the world.

Decentralization of decision making entails delegation to country managers and this, by definition, carries some risk. In fact, all delegation is a tradeoff between efficiency and risk. In delegating decision making to country managers, we run the risk that the global (or headquarters-based) interests of the corporation will not be taken into account. This concern is well illustrated in the case of KFC in Japan, the case that began this chapter. Other risks are that country managers will make decisions with arbitrary, egotistical, or capricious motives. The case of KFC, although this time in Hong Kong, can serve again as an example here:

> Hong Kong is a perfect example of what not to do. They sent an insensitive and patronizing Australian who saw himself as a high-powered corporate executive. He breezed in, hired a secretary, bought a Mercedes, and immediately began driving around to inspect potential sites. There was no effort to understand local tastes or customs. He paid exorbitant prices for the sites, entered a joint venture with, of all parties, a UK-based conglomerate, and set up standard stores with standard menus. When stores opened, he was not close to the operations and wasn't even aware that the fish meal-fed chicken he was buying had a strong unpleasant taste. It was a total disaster.[10]

Continued questions for headquarters of multinational firms include: How do we know that the decisions implemented by foreign subsidiaries (e.g. people recruited, commercial strategy for entering markets, choice of locations) are the best for the firm? Were there other options left unexplored? Have country managers invested the required effort and did they have enough information to make the best possible decision for the firm? In short, how can we evaluate or verify the quality of the country managers' decisions to ensure that those decisions are in line with our interests?

The tradeoff between efficiency and risk of the delegation to the country managers is typically studied under the economic theory known as agency theory.[11] The headquarters, or principal, designates a country manager, or agent, to guard its interests; but the country manager may make decisions based on his or her own interests, which may not coincide with those of headquarters. Thus, the problem for headquarters is how to control or ensure that the decisions made by the country manager are congruent with its own interests and objectives. The possible incongruence of objectives between headquarters and the subsidiary "goes with the territory" in multinational firms and is not limited to KFC. Table 7.1 includes

Table 7.1   Goal Incongruence between HQs and Subsidiary Managers: Some Additional Examples

---

In 1994, Ford Motor Company launched a program for ideas and suggestions that would permit subsidiaries to exchange experiences and improvements among one another. The program was introduced in the US and in Ford's subsidiary electronics plants in Canada, Mexico, and Brazil. However, the country managers of other subsidiaries (e.g. the one in Spain) put up a great deal of resistance and stood in the way of implementation in their territories. They preferred to maintain their own systems, which had been designed with the help of local consultants.[12]

In the early 1990s, when Jan Timmer was CEO of the Dutch electronics company Philips, he put into place a drastic cost reduction program that resulted in the dismissal of 68 000 workers, earning Timmer the nickname "The Butcher of Eindhoven." Many country managers refused to follow this directive and did their best to "dig in their heels to save local jobs."[13]

The enormous autonomy of Procter & Gamble's subsidiaries during the 1980s impeded the global rollout of new products and technology improvements. Country managers often resisted such initiatives because they would have a negative impact on their particular subsidiary's success. As a consequence, the commercial release of several new products was delayed by a decade or more.[14]

During the 1990s, the CEO of the Japanese company Matsushita, Toshihito Yamashita, adopted a series of initiatives to empower innovation in the company's foreign subsidiaries, which involved transferring many resources and responsibilities to these subsidiaries (e.g. the plant in Cardiff, Wales). In an unprecedented move for a Japanese CEO, Yamashita publicly expressed his displeasure at Cardiff's lack of initiative in fulfilling the task he had entrusted them with.[15]

---

some examples of incongruity of objectives in other major companies. As this table illustrates, the relationship between headquarters and foreign subsidiaries may be fraught with conflicts.

Even excluding cases of incompetence or opportunism,[16] incongruence of objectives may be a natural result of the different perspectives that typically exist between headquarters and subsidiaries. While headquarters is concerned with the corporation as a whole, the essential mission of country managers is often to optimize the results and performance of their own subsidiary. As is shown in the examples of Table 7.1, the two goals do not always align. To try to ensure that subsidiaries act in accord with the objectives of headquarters, there are three instruments or basic forms of control: monitoring, incentives, and socialization. We will briefly examine each of these.

Monitoring. Monitoring centers on the actions and decisions of the subsidiary. This control of behavior or conduct can be exercised by very different methods such as restricting the subsidiary's margin of autonomy or discretion and obligating it to operate in a certain manner. This set of monitoring practices is often referred to as *operating control*. Operating control imposes rules, operating procedures, performance reviews, or standards that specify what the subsidiary must accomplish. Generally, operating control is exercised over factors that are specifically strategic for the firm. For example, the distinctive competitive advantage of the Spanish fashion chain Zara[17] resides in completing its process of production, from the design of the garments through their distribution to the stores, in less than 15 days; this allows stores to completely update their merchandise in this same time period, a factor which, along with price and design, is critical in the fashion industry. The company controls all the essential elements to maintain this distinctive advantage, emphasizing the need to ensure, throughout the company's worldwide network, certain very precise norms in terms of product mix, marketing information systems, and inventory control. Outside of these norms, the local managers at Zara enjoy an ample margin of autonomy and discretion for adapting the work system to conditions in their local market. In this way, while we encounter the same products, the same target market segment, and an identical policy of inventory rotation throughout the company's worldwide network of stores, many other elements, such as internal communication policies, sales promotions, or merchandising may differ among different subsidiaries.

A second form of control is *administrative control*. Audits, approval forms, and local market analyses prepared for headquarters are examples of this form of monitoring. These reports are an attempt by headquarters to obtain more information about the subsidiary's activities in order to evaluate the quality of the decisions being made for the overall good of the firm. This is a type of control very commonly used in multinational firms but is, however, often insufficient. Based on the geographic distance often separating subsidiaries from headquarters, some subsidiaries managers may be able to work around the administrative controls by covering up numbers in their budget estimates, submitting approval forms after the corresponding decisions are already made, or writing reports designed more to placate headquarters than to execute an exhaustive and rigorous analysis of their market. These possibilities cannot be excluded *a priori*.

A third form of monitoring is *strategic control*. This control can be realized by means of on-site visits by managers from headquarters, but also through expatriate managers who are placed as country managers within the subsidiaries. As expatriates from headquarters are presumed to embody the "headquarters way" of doing things, they bring a piece of headquarters' oversight to the foreign subsidiary. In their control function, these expatriate country managers ensure that the strategic decisions in the subsidiary conform to the interests and culture of the organization, and supply headquarters with information about the local market.

It is important that these different forms of monitoring do not suffocate any subsidiary's entrepreneurial spirit. This entrepreneurial freedom in decision making may be especially important in the first stages of the subsidiary's existence, when a great deal of flexibility and initiative is needed in order to adapt the company's products and policies to the local market. Imposing many controls can not only distract and overload local managers, but can also end up impeding their ability to do their jobs efficiently. As we saw in our example of Zara, it is essential that monitoring only cover the strategic aspects of the operation and that it be complemented with other forms of control. As always, managing the global workforce is often about striking the necessary balance between the local subsidiary's needs and headquarters-based needs.

Incentives. Monitoring is not always the most effective control mechanism. It is not the best, for example, when there is a marked asymmetry of information (e.g. the subsidiary possesses much more information and knowledge about what works and what needs to be done in the local environment). Various factors can create asymmetries of information. One is cultural distance. As discussed earlier, different countries have different characteristics and values which can oblige us to behave in very different ways. The greater the cultural difference between the home country and the subsidiary, the more difficult it will be to judge the extent to which certain decisions respond to the need to adapt to local idiosyncrasies, or are motivated by opportunism (in the sense of the theory mentioned earlier).

The type of subsidiary also has an influence on the asymmetry of information. In some cases, headquarters has a vision and a reasonable amount of specific knowledge of what the subsidiary needs to be doing. For example, the traditional strategy of Matsushita has been to design and produce relatively standard products on a large scale and export them from Japan to the rest of the world. The role of each subsidiary is to help headquarters to implement this strategy inside of its particular geographic territory. In this context, headquarters is sufficiently familiar with the subsidiaries' mission to evaluate the quality of their performance on reasonable grounds. In fact, it was a habitual practice in Matsushita to evaluate the managers of its exterior divisions with identical criteria and to replace them if they saw the operational profits of their unit fall to less than 4 % of sales for two consecutive years.[18]

There are other cases, of course, where the subsidiary has much more information or more advanced or specialized knowledge than headquarters, as occurred in the case of Procter & Gamble's Japanese subsidiary. Knowing that the Japanese consumer is particularly demanding when it comes to personal care products, this subsidiary was motivated to propose dozens of very competitive ideas and products which were eventually transferred to other subsidiaries of P&G.[19] In these cases, the best thing headquarters could do was to allow the subsidiary to act in accordance with its own initiative, without interfering or requiring it to conduct its business in certain ways.

The challenge remains for multinationals of how to control subsidiaries in the presence of an asymmetrical amount of information. Many multinationals will allow their subsidiaries to exercise control over themselves, through a series of rewards and incentives. In this case, incentives should be designed to align the interests of headquarters and the subsidiary. In this way, if a proportion of the salary of the subsidiary's top management is based on the subsidiary's results in the context of the organization's results, the members of the subsidiary's top management team (who may have been otherwise motivated to pursue their own interests) will be motivated to work for the best interests of headquarters.

While incentives are certainly an excellent mechanism for aligning interests multiple studies have shown that they are not always efficient.[20] There are two factors that make incentives successful as management tools. They are the extent to which outcomes can be (1) measured and (2) controlled. Outcome measurability is the degree to which outcomes are specific and quantifiable. Outcome controllability is the degree to which a clear connection exists between effort and outcomes. In general, the clearer and easier to measure the outcomes are, and the fewer variables outside of the employee's control are present in the job, the more effective incentives will be as a motivating tool.

Unfortunately, in the environment of multinationals, these two ideal conditions do not always exist. Outcomes may be unclear, contradictory, or poorly specified[21] such as those objectives that consist of improving relations with a national government or improving the perception of the firm in the local market. It is not easy to measure the attainment of these kinds of objectives. And the more difficult it is to measure a given outcome, the more difficult it is to decide on the appropriateness of awarding compensation or bonuses associated with its attainment. Furthermore, objectives often appear and evolve through many and complicated interactions among the parties. For example, the Swiss company Schindler entrusted a young Italian expatriate, Silvio Napoli, with implementing the company's entry strategy in India.[22] This strategy was centered upon two elements: introducing a line of standardized elevators to the Indian market, and sourcing most of the components locally. After several months, this strategy encountered so many difficulties that the company began a process of redefining its objectives. Moreover, in the summer of Schindler's first year of being established in India, the Indian government passed a new budget that included increased import duties on specific noncore goods, including elevators. This uncontrollable factor was devastating to the enterprise and very frustrating for Napoli, who found it impossible to achieve the break-even objectives that had been set for him.

In an incentive system, the managers of a subsidiary may be forced to assume a great deal of risk, particularly when there are circumstances beyond the employees' control (e.g. absence of local reputation for the company, industry volatility, lack of economic or political stability in the country). Given that people tend to be risk-averse, in such circumstances we will very probably see ourselves obligated to offer a greater reward to compensate such executives for the greater risk they must assume.

Socialization. Consistent with agency theory, businesses, both domestic and multinational, are collections of individuals who learn to cooperate for reasons of self-interest. This perspective emphasizes the potential conflicts of interest among members of the group (which is, by definition, the problem of agency) and underplays other concepts such as identity, socialization, and leadership. Individuals are not motivated solely by self-interest. Individuals' behavior is also explained by norms of loyalty, reciprocity, professional pride, or the desire to maintain traditions. Consider, for example, the challenge of recruiting satisfied employees from other companies or the pride one may feel after hearing one's company president give a motivating speech.

Introducing controls and offering incentives is necessary, as we have seen, to prevent the problems that arise from a possible incongruence of objectives across subsidiaries in a multinational company. However, there may be a more interpersonally effective way to also encourage congruence – through socialization. Effective socialization encourages employees to see their organization's values and mission as their own.[23] Effective socialization promotes those management objectives which lead employees to identify with their organization and contribute to its success.

As we discussed in Chapter 5, one tactic that effectively encourages the socialization of managers from various subsidiaries into sharing headquarters' values and mission is the placement of inpatriates. Inpatriates are a variation on the expatriate employee in that the inpatriate is working out of his or her home country – but working in headquarters. In other words, local nationals are brought to headquarters to learn the company way of doing things – and to then be ambassadors back in their subsidiary after their time as an inpatriate. They are, in many ways, expected to be socializing agents. Inpatriates may be placed in county manager positions or other positions of presumed influence within the subsidiary. One of the key benefits of inpatriates is that they are able to learn the corporate values of the MNC but simultaneously function fluently within the local environment. As a result, they are particularly suited to blend global integration with local responsiveness.

7.2.3   Encouraging Cooperation among Subsidiaries

In the previous section we described how to encourage country managers to perform well within the scope of their subsidiary and align their attitudes and behaviors for the overall good of the organization. As we have discussed, country managers have responsibilities for their units' performance – a local mission – but they must also contribute to improving the corporation's overall competitive position – a global mission. Sometimes, as we saw in Chapter 2, what is developed and implemented in one country can also be very useful in another country. Let's consider the following two anecdotes regarding the cooperation across entities within the firm:

"When we were discussing the business plan with Mr. Schindler, he said, 'India will be our Formula One racing track.' In the auto industry, 90 % of all innovations are developed for and tested on Formula One cars and then reproduced on a much larger scale and adapted for the mass market. We are testing things in India – in isolation and on a fast track – that probably could not be done anywhere else in the company. The expectation is that what we prove can be adapted to the rest of the group." Silvio Napoli, Country Manager for India, Schindler Limited[24]

"The opportunity to compete in one of the world's most advanced markets is without a doubt one of the reasons why we were keen to enter the U.K. All of the [major] banks are here and the market is very demanding, with some highly sophisticated financial products. In the same way, as our managers have brought many things from Spain, like the commercial policy or the client relationships, we expect that other locations will also be able to capitalize on what they learn and implement here." Javier Bugallo, HR Director, Grupo Santander, London[25]

Multinationals also have a challenge to identify and disseminate the best ideas and practices within the corporation, regardless of where they originate. Although this is undoubtedly a noble and desirable objective, it is certainly not an easy one to fulfill. Many barriers intervene and impede the transfer of knowledge and best practices among the various units of the multinational (see Chapter 2). It is useful to identify and take action against two barriers that stand in the way of this objective becoming a reality:

• The subsidiary that originates an idea may be reluctant to share the knowledge and experience that have contributed to its success. If this is the case, consider the alignment of incentives; if the country managers are compensated for the results attained by the subsidiary, why would they choose to dedicate time, personnel, and resources to showing others something from which they will not derive any benefit?
• Those subsidiaries receiving an idea from another subsidiary may not be motivated to accept it. This tends to be particularly prevalent in subsidiaries that have enjoyed a great deal of autonomy. What incentives are in place to encourage the receipt and sharing of knowledge and ideas?

It is important, as we consider the best ways to manage the global workforce, that we reduce the motivational barriers preventing cooperation among organizational units around the world. The research literature suggests two ways to create a climate of cooperation among the corporate units: through rewards policies and through programs of corporate integration.

Rewards policies. Traditional reward systems have a tendency to reward those who produce or achieve results rather than those who share for others to achieve results. This has important implications for encouraging cooperation among subsidiaries. If an individual is rewarded for what he or she knows that his or her colleagues do not, then sharing and disseminating knowledge will have a cost for him or her. It is essential to create a climate in which the individual is rewarded for sharing experience, ideas, and knowledge.

One method of promoting this climate is through monetary incentives which reward cooperation or sharing. There are at least two basic referent units to which the variable component of the salary can be linked: the corporation and the subsidiary. Selection of the referent unit will have a strong influence on the degree of the subsidiary managers' cooperation with other units and on the unit to which they will be most committed. As mentioned, if they are paid exclusively in terms of their own unit's performance, they will have no incentive to do anything but maximize their local profitability. In contrast, if a significant percentage of total compensation is linked to the corporation's overall results, they will have a clear incentive to disseminate knowledge and information to other units. While monetary rewards are often used, it is important to recognize that these benefits may be realized with non-monetary rewards as well. The rewards of career and professional development can also create an adequate climate for motivating individuals to share their experiences within the multinational network. Thus, it is important to design international career path frameworks where those who collaborate and share knowledge effectively across subsidiaries are those who are promoted to progressively more global roles.

Corporate integration programs. To create a climate of cooperation it is also important to promote a common vision and shared values. To this end, multinational companies need to encourage interaction, making use of two essential mechanisms of integration:[26]

- *Vertical integration mechanisms.* These consist of facilitating contact and communication with headquarters so that it will be aware of the interests of the overall corporation and the role of each subsidiary. Examples of such mechanisms include the temporary assignment of inpatriates, or subsidiary employees, to positions at headquarters, corporate training programs, and providing subsidiary managers with a mentor at headquarters.
- *Lateral integration mechanisms.* These are activities and initiatives that facilitate contact among employees and managers at parallel levels in the various subsidiaries of a multinational organization. Multinational product development work teams, for example, can be formed to eliminate unnecessary differences in products from one country to another, reduce the duplication of effort in product development, and gain consensus on the diffusion of new products and services. In addition, the corporation can hold global training meetings and activities with participation from different subsidiaries around the world.

In sum, facilitating cooperation across subsidiaries involves facilitating networking among people from diverse countries, encouraging interactions, and information sharing among the various business units. In the absence of such integration mechanisms, subsidiaries are neither forced to learn from nor expected to contribute to the rest of the organization. To limit barriers to cooperation, we should manage the global workforce in ways that will encourage cross-national learning and the interchange of experiences, ideas, and information across foreign subsidiaries.

7.3   Motivating International Assignees

As described in this chapter, compensation and reward systems are key elements in motivating attitudes and behaviors within the workforce. Designing compensation and rewards systems for international assignees is particularly complex and difficult given that they need to take into account a set of situational factors not normally encountered in a strictly domestic context. Let's consider just a few of the factors which complicate international assignees' compensation and rewards: the nationality or home location of the international assignee; his or her family situation (number and ages of children, work situation of the spouse); exchange rates; differences in living costs, taxes, and inflation rates; the need to reconcile home and host country laws and regulations for compensation and benefits; and the geographically imposed problems of communication and control. While these issues make the compensation and rewards of international assignees more challenging, their attitudes and behaviors (as we have seen in the examples of expatriate country managers and inpatriates) may be critical for the integration of the firm globally. Let's consider these both further.

7.3.1   Compensating International Assignees

To develop an "ideal" compensation system for international assignees, we must consider whether the system we are developing will achieve the following five objectives:

1. To attract international assignees to accept positions in the areas where we have our greatest needs and opportunities;
2. To facilitate the transfer of employees across national units in the most cost-effective manner;
3. To facilitate re-entry into the home country or redeployment to another subsidiary at the end of the international assignment;

4. To be consistent and fair in the treatment of international assignees, and not generate counterproductive (or resentful) behaviors among local employees; and

5. To encourage international assignees to do their best and apply all of their abilities (e.g. knowledge, creativity, relationship-
building) to help achieve the company's business strategy.

Taken individually, these objectives seem logical and achievable.
However, the implementation of one may, in fact, contradict or
impede the successful execution of others.

Let us suppose, for example, that we have an excellent plan of
international expansion and we want to attract key talent for this
endeavor. It is likely, despite our best efforts in offering an attractive
compensation package, that some of our best candidates will, for
various reasons unrelated to our offer, refuse the assignment. They
may have a family situation which precludes them from accepting
the assignment (e.g. a school-age child with special needs, a spouse's
career, a family member's unwillingness to move), or they may refuse
because they perceive the destination country to be too dangerous
or unattractive for some reason. Candidates may refuse offers for
international assignments because they are concerned about what
will happen to their careers after they return home (e.g. whether their
experience will be valued or whether they will receive the position
to which they aspire), or because they believe their opportunities
for promotion will be better if they remain at headquarters where
they are visible among senior leaders. Research has found that all
of these reasons, unrelated to compensation, will influence whether
one is willing to accept an international assignment.[27]

While these reasons for refusing assignments are unrelated to
compensation, compensation is often used as the motivator to over-
come them. This increased compensation sometimes works to con-
vince candidates to accept assignments, but, in doing so, companies
may need to abandon one of the other objectives mentioned above.
For example, increasing compensation as a method of recruitment
leads to excessively costly assignments, violating the "most cost-
effective" provision of our second objective. Increasing compensation may also conflict with the third objective (i.e. repatriation) by
encouraging international assignees to remain on assignment because they will not be able to maintain their excessively high compensation after the assignment. Finally, the generous international

assignee compensation designed to help attract otherwise reticent candidates will likely have the effect of creating large pay gaps between international assignees and local employees. The comparatively poorly compensated host country nationals may perceive their company to have unfair procedural and distributive justice. Thus, the company fails to achieve the fourth objective, fairness. As this example illustrates, there may be tradeoffs among objectives when compensating international assignees and these tradeoffs need to be fully considered by HR professionals developing the practices.

In order to establish the salary of international assignees, the first thing we need to do is choose a referent salary. The referent salary is the comparison salary used as the basis for calculating all international assignee incentives, salary differentials, and allowances. There are three possibilities when selecting a referent salary: (1) establish the assignee's salary in the context of the destination (host country), (2) establish the assignee's salary in the context of a global system, or (3) establish the assignee's salary in the context of the assignee's country of origin. Each of these possibilities has strengths and weaknesses.

Host country approach. In the host country approach, the compensation goal is to fit the international assignee into the host country salary structure. In some cases this approach may be useful and viable, especially if a number of eligible candidates for the particular position have a personal interest in living in a given location, and the local salary does not seem unattractive. This method is generally not viable when we attempt to use it on assignees going to host countries that are considered unattractive or to host countries where the standard of living is lower than that of the country of origin.

Global approach. In the global approach, the compensation goal is to fit the international assignee into one company-wide standard, irrespective of their home country or the country to which they will be assigned. Incentives and allowances will be derived from that common base. This approach works particularly well with international assignees expected to move to more than one host country, thereby losing any direct connection with either their home country or any single host country's grading and pay structure.

Home country approach. In the home country approach, the compensation goal is to provide the expatriate with equivalent purchasing power abroad that he or she enjoyed in his or her home country. This approach is often referred to as the balance sheet approach.

With this approach, global HR professionals need to apply home country deductions and pay differential allowances (cost of living differential, housing allowance) to arrive at a net disposable income which should maintain the expatriate's home country standard of living.

According to the Worldwide Survey of International Assignment Policies and Practices, conducted by the ORC,[28] the home country approach is the dominant method of determining compensation for international assignees; it is the common practice among 70 % of European, 65 % of Asian, and 79 % of North American companies. It is popular for several reasons: By keeping expatriates' pay in line with conditions at home, companies can avoid having to face great discrepancies when the assignees return to their home country after their international assignment. In addition, it will help the company achieve worldwide consistency in its expatriate employment practices. This approach, while popular, has its drawbacks, especially when assignees of different nationalities work together in similar jobs.[29] This approach is also expensive, especially for assignees of some nationalities. For example, American expatriates are usually subject to higher income taxes abroad. The maximum marginal rate in the US is 31 %, compared with 65 % in Japan, 53 % in Germany, and 45 % in Spain. Maintaining the same level of net salary entails receiving an even higher level of gross salary. Firms using this approach need to carry that additional cost as part of the assignment terms.

Once the referent salary is determined using whatever method the company prefers, the next step is to add a series of additional elements to form the typical international assignee's compensation package. These elements may include: cost of living and housing allowances, foreign service premiums (i.e. mobility premium, hardship pay), income tax reimbursements, support programs (e.g. children's education, shipping and storage of goods, travel, club memberships), and performance incentives. In Table 7.2, we include the prevalence of these elements in international assignee compensation packages.

Data from Table 7.2 help explain why expatriation is an expensive staffing approach. The average compensation package of international assignees is between two to five times as much as that received by their counterparts at home, and a great deal more than that received by the local nationals in the developing countries.[30] For instance, it was estimated that international assignees in China

Table 7.2 Compensation Components in European MNCs

Elements	European MNCs n = 187
Cost of living and housing allowances	
Cost of living Allowance/COLA	86 %
Housing	
Free assignment housing	44 %
Other (for example, housing differential)	48 %
Foreign service premiums	
Mobility premium	
For moves within the same continent	56 %
For moves from one continent to another	60 %
Hardship pay	57 %
Income tax reimbursments	
Tax policy	
Tax equalize	65 %
Tax protection	8 %
Tax free	4 %
Other (for example, laissez-faire)	23 %
Assistance programs	
Education allowance	
Always	44 %
If no suitable free education is available	47 %
Shipping and storage cost	
Shipping costs	96 %
Storage costs	75 %
First or Business Class air travel	
For senior management	49 %
Other expatriates	19 %
Club membership	
For senior management	59 %
Other expatriates	39 %
Performance incentives	93 %

Source: Based on 2002 Worldwide Survey of International Assignment Policies and Practices, European Edition, Organization Resources Counselors.

at the beginning of this century earned between 20 and 50 times more than local employees.[31] Likewise, in a survey conducted by The Conference Board, more than two-thirds of the 152 respondents reported that expatriates cost at least three times their salary. The managerial questions are whether these higher costs of staffing with expatriates are justified and whether the negative influence of pay disparities between expatriates and host country nationals are worth the sense of inequity that may be created.

7.3.2 Justifying the Costs of International Assignees

We must expect that, especially in times of economic crisis, businesses will need to reduce their use of expatriates in order to cut costs. In the 2003/2004 Global Relocation Survey, 64 % of the 134 company respondents indicated that their companies were reducing international assignment expenses in response to current economic conditions.[32] The way these companies cut back on expatriates did vary. Some companies opted to send only the most essential associates on expatriate assignments. Some companies opted to reduce the duration of the assignments. Other companies reduced allowances, adopted the host country approach, or increased the recruitment of local personnel.

All of these approaches can make perfect sense in a business context that requires maximum efficiency. These cost-saving techniques, however, are concerning for three reasons. First, costs must always be counterbalanced by benefits. As we saw in Chapter 6, international assignments can allow us to transfer valuable knowledge and experience from country to country, assure that the adaptation to local conditions in subsidiaries does not take place at the expense of headquarters, and develop the global talent and leadership required for the future of the organization.[33] Admittedly, all of these functions have a cost, but we should not lose sight of the strategic role international assignees can play – because this loss would also be a cost to the organization. From the Global Relocations Study mentioned earlier, it is not surprising that a high percentage (82 %) of respondents prepared cost estimates before assignments, and 81 % tracked these costs during the assignment. However, only 10 % of respondents reported that they measured the impact of international assignments on the bottom line. Costs, for those firms not associating international assignees' contributions with benefits, would be reduced only by reducing the number of expatriates. This is both unfortunate and short-sighted for multinational firms.

The second concern is when local nationals are hired as a cost-saving approach, with little regard for the strategic gains that might be lost by not having a boundary-spanning international assignee in a given role. In deciding whether to recruit a local manager or an expatriate to fill a managerial position, relative salary levels are not the only economic items involved. Instead, we need to consider the total costs associated, both tangible and strategic, and opt for the one which minimizes total costs. Research has shown[34] that during the first stages of expansion into a country, especially when there is a greater cultural distance, the use of international assignees involves a lower level of "total" costs and, therefore, can be a cost-effective solution.

The third concern is that reducing costs through fewer inter-national assignees ignores the other possibility of the cost–benefit equation. That is, maximizing benefits may be achieved by increas-ing contributions. Many organizations put themselves under pres-sure to reduce salary costs without adequately exploring how to opti-mize international assignees' contributions. We recommend paying more attention to the design of incentive systems that encourage expatriates to do their best and to provide the type of discretionary effort required by their job. If this is not done, in spite of all the rhetoric about the value of international experience, international assignees will be regarded not as an investment, but purely as a cost.

7.3.3   The Consequences of Expatriate Compensation on Host Nationals

The pay differentials, premiums, and allowances included in the typi-cal expatriate compensation package are generally far more gener-ous when compared to the compensation of equivalently placed host country nationals (i.e. those host nationals with similar responsibil-ities, doing comparable work, and expending comparable effort). In an effort to leverage the boundary-spanning abilities of international assignees the consequent pay disparity between expatriates and their host national counterparts is often ignored. It should not be ignored; it is well documented that the perception of salary injustice usually leads to a series of undesirable work attitudes and behaviors such as reduced commitment, reduced collaboration, greater turnover and absenteeism and, in sum, poorer performance.

If host national employees appear to be unfairly treated in relation to the expatriates, they will likely give little support to collaboration, which will make it difficult for the expatriates to adapt and perform. It is important that we look beyond the expatriates' viewpoint and begin assessing the potential impact of expatriate pay on host nationals' attitudes. To accomplish this, we can rely on equity theory which will be summarized briefly below.

The principal proponents of equity theory were Eliot Jaques and John Stacy Adams who, in the 1960s, analyzed the conditions that explain salary dissatisfaction.[35] Although there are minor differences between them, they both concur that when individuals evaluate their salary fairness, they apply at least two ratios.

1. The ratio of contributions (inputs) to rewards (outcomes). Among the inputs individuals include their comprehensive investments, such as intelligence, education, skills, and experience, and specific work actions needed for task fulfillment. Among the outcomes, individuals include all the inducements, money, esteem, status, and the like that employees receive from the organization. The value of one's exchange with the organization depends on this input–outcome ratio.
2. The salary which we receive in relation to that of others. Individuals judge the fairness of their exchange relationships with the organization by comparing the balance between our inputs and outcomes to the input and outcome ratios we perceive in our referent groups. Dissimilar ratios lead to perceptions of inequity.

We make these social comparisons against a variety of referents, both internal and external. Internal referents are persons holding similar positions within the same organization, whereas external referents are typically those holding similar jobs in other organizations. In sum, the source of our salary dissatisfaction may not necessarily be the absolute quantity of the salary we obtain, but the salary we receive in relation to that of others and in relation to the balance between contributions and rewards.

This analysis can easily be extended to the case of salary disparity between expatriates and host country nationals.[36] The establishment of more generous pay conditions for expatriates violates the norm of equity, which assumes that employees are most content when their input–outcome ratio resembles that of their referents. Host country nationals who adhere to this norm will perceive themselves to be under-rewarded. We can also expect that, in general, the larger the pay differential between host country nationals and expatriates holding similar jobs, the higher the perception of pay unfairness among the host country nationals.

There are some variables that moderate the perception of inequity that salary disparity causes, or make it more (or less) justifiable in the eyes of local employees. We will briefly analyze each of these variables.

Expatriates' contributions and needs. Receiving identical outcomes is not always considered the fairest solution. There are two rules of distribution that support the justification of unequal outcomes: the *contribution rule*, in which individuals are rewarded in proportion to their inputs; and the *needs rule*, in which individuals are rewarded on the basis of their legitimate needs. If a local employee believes that the expatriate with whom he or she works contributes more (e.g. has more experience, abilities, or more and better contacts than he or she has), the rule of contribution helps host country nationals perceive the higher compensation to be fair. If, on the contrary, the expatriate fits the profile of the ineffective KFC Hong Kong executive we mentioned earlier, the host country national may find the salary disparity intolerable.

If host country nationals perceive the expatriates' financial needs to be greater, the rule of necessity can make us view the disparity in salary as legitimate. One may perceive these greater needs if the expatriate has had to make certain sacrifices in order to adapt to the new country. For example, one might discover that the expatriate's spouse had to give up his or her job, or that the children required special attention. One might also believe that the expatriates come from a more developed country and therefore require a higher salary to maintain the same standard of living they enjoyed at home. Higher expatriate rewards are deemed to be justified to compensate for additional expenses (e.g. housing, travel) and risks (e.g. repatriation, being away from headquarters) that they would not be subjected to if they had stayed at home.

Interpersonal sensitivity. Organizational justice research has shown that treating people with dignity and respect increases their perceptions of fairness and the likelihood of accepting outcomes, both positive and negative.[37] Interpersonally sensitive and effective expatriates will be held in higher esteem and host country nationals will downplay the importance of the salary differences that exist. In contrast, the perception of the pay discrepancy may be exacerbated when expatriates act in a contemptuous, cold, or arrogant manner.

Perceived advantage over other host country nationals. It is hard to imagine anyone that wants to feel mistreated. It provokes tension, and tension motivates individuals to seek relief. To relieve this tension, caused by feeling as though one is being unfairly compensated, one can leave the organization, stay but reduce one's inputs (i.e. effort in the job), or change the social referents until a more comparably favorable group is found. The latter would include host country nationals who compare themselves to lesser paid host country nationals in comparable positions but with other companies.

Degree of interaction with international assignee. The degree of closeness or interaction between expatriates and local employees varies. Expatriates may work side-by-side with host country nationals or may appear only occasionally to perform some specific task. If contact with expatriates is very close, host county nationals will likely have more information about the expatriates' compensation at their disposal, either directly or indirectly through observation. Close contact with similarly qualified expatriates will also increase their salience, thereby increasing the likelihood that the expatriates are the referent group for pay equity purposes. All of this will serve to increase the perception of inequity. Thus, it is likely that the perception of inequity will be more prevalent when a close and permanent relationship exists than when such contact is only occasional.

In sum, we cannot expect locals to understand and justify the salary disparity that separates them from their expatriate counterparts if:

- the expatriates do not contribute more;
- do not appear to have greater needs;
- their treatment of colleagues is insensitive or not culturally appropriate; and
- above all, if frequent interaction with them makes the disparity constantly present in the host nationals' minds.

Firms cannot have a suitable international assignment policy unless they take these factors into account and try to mitigate them whenever possible.

7.3.4 *Other Issues in Motivating International Assignees*

Individuals can be motivated by means other than compensation to accept a global assignment and, once they are in the foreign location, be willing to do their best. Two of these reasons that are normally important are: the desire to have an international experience and the desire to improve in one's professional career.

International job experience. When we speak with people working abroad, it is not difficult for us to get them to comment on many negative or problematic aspects of their experience. They will probably talk about culture shock, family adjustment problems, stress, having to travel a lot, the sensation of isolation, and so forth. But they will also typically bring up many positive aspects of their experience. The experience will undoubtedly have both sunshine and shadows. But which areas tend to have the most sunshine, and which the most shadows? In an empirical study, Guzzo, Noonan, and Elron[38] asked what distinguished positive and negative aspects of working abroad. They classified the responses into three categories, according to whether they were related to the work itself, family, or life in general. They found that in the third category (i.e. life in general), positive and negative experiences were very much equal. Many of the negative aspects mentioned had to do with the family (e.g. family disruption or stress, partner dissatisfaction). In contrast, on the positive side were many factors having to do with the work: more motivating job, skill building, learning and growth, network development, and so forth.

It is not surprising that expatriates (at least those in management positions) find their work motivating. We are reminded of the case of Silvio Napoli, whom we mentioned earlier. Recall that the employer Schindler sent Napoli to open a subsidiary in India. What could he expect in this destination? Like many other expatriates in similar situations, Napoli would carry a heavy workload, most likely experience difficulties adapting, and would have to define the specific content of his duties little by little as he went along. All of these elements would generate stress for him and likely have a negative influence on his work satisfaction. However, it is also true that in this job he would have an immense experience of personal and professional learning and growth; enjoy enormous independence and discretion to make decisions and decide how to do his job; exercise many different duties requiring a range of skills, abilities, and talents; assume responsibility in a highly relevant and visible task; and have the possibility of building a strongly results-oriented work environment. All of these characteristics of his position contributed to the fact that, in the end and not without difficulties, Napoli would have a satisfactory global work experience. In fact, many of the characteristics which Hackman and Oldham[39] included to explain what motivates individuals in their jobs were realized: skill variety, autonomy, task identity, task significance, and feedback. If these characteristics are present in the particular foreign position being assigned, we can expect that it will be a highly motivating job for the person.

Career prospects. Let's continue with the case of Silvio Napoli. What motivated him to accept the assignment and to contribute his best efforts to it was not so much the challenge it posed as the possibilities for promotion within the company that would be open to him. He believed that if he succeeded in his assignment in India, he would be assigned to other positions of greater responsibility at Schindler. And, in fact, this came true. As we were told in an update to the case, "in 2005 Napoli moved to Hong Kong to first take the position as Managing Director Schindler, Hong Kong and later during the same year the position of CEO of Jardine Schindler Group, a Joint Venture between Jardine Matheson and Schindler Group of Switzerland."

For an assignment to lead to a promotion is not, however, as frequent an occurrence as the case of Silvio Napoli may suggest. As we saw in Chapter 6, research from the 1980s and 90s consistently showed that, for repatriates who stayed in the same organization, international assignments did not always have a positive impact. Lack of respect for acquired skills, loss of status, and reverse culture shock were reported to be recurring problems for repatriates. The Global Relocation Trends Survey indicated that this tendency had not changed: nearly half (40 %) of the 134 respondents indicated that they were "not sure" about the value of international experience for an expatriate's career, and only 34 % indicated that international assignments help expatriates to be promoted faster.

The outcome of an international assignment varies by person, company, and assignment. In order for one to advance more quickly in one's organization, a series of circumstances need to be present.[40] For example, one needs to do a good job and fulfill the expectations of upper management; the subsidiary or unit where one is assigned needs to be strategically important; one's business needs to have a clear mission and international presence; upper management needs to promote and value international experience; and management mechanisms need to exist such that the assignments turn out well (e.g. international career plans, mentoring, support programs).

Of course, all of these circumstances are not always present. Does that mean that if what you truly want is to advance in your career, your best (or most secure) bet is to forget about acquiring international experience? We would not like to come to this conclusion. And indeed, recent research[41] suggests that, at least for those who aspire to attain a top management position and financial advantages, having international experience is becoming more and more important. In particular, it has shown that international experience does, in fact, increase opportunities for a top management position and for a better salary, even though that position and that salary may not be in the same organization where the international assignment occurred. If the company where you work does not value what you have learned and developed in your foreign assignment, there are probably others who will.

Performance management. There are some challenges when considering the performance evaluation of international assignees living and working outside of their own national borders. Considering that an international assignment is a job context and not a job description, it is important for organizations to determine the specific objective and subjective performance dimensions for each of their international assignees respectively. Technical performance tends to be objective and generally includes those behaviors that either transform raw material into goods or services, or otherwise directly support an organization's technical core.[42] More subjective performance dimensions may include aspects such as team work, managing with integrity, continuous learning, and the like. Performance management for international assignees should also include a consideration of whether developmental or strategic assignees have been successful with their developmental goals. These developmental goals are often in the area of broadening international business knowledge, developing a global network of colleagues, developing cultural agility – which enables success in leading teams, negotiating, etc. in multiple cultural contexts. We recommend that HR professionals design performance instruments for international assignees that best reflect the objective, subjective, and developmental dimensions of a given assignment.

Once the appropriate performance dimensions have been identified for the various international assignments within a multinational organization, international assignees' supervisors should then be trained to use the dimensions to assess assignees' performance, whether on global or local standards (depending on the firm strategy again). Some performance dimensions of international assignees' jobs will be the same regardless of their national location; however, the way in which these tasks are conducted and assessed in performance management may be different as a result of the host country context.

7.4 Chapter Conclusions

The principles and tools for motivating people in different cultural environments are very important for helping a firm realize its global business strategy. There is great diversity across cultures in how employees should be motivated and their attitudes and behaviors shaped. In general, human resource professionals and managers in global firms should consider the following points.

Do not assume a one best way to motivate employees. The effectiveness of a particular motivation practice depends on how well it matches a national value system. This should lead you to avoid the temptation of using identical motivation tools across the different cultural environments in which you operate. This is certainly progress compared with the ethnocentric and arrogant mentality of earlier times.

Ensure that the attitudes and behaviors within the subsidiaries are well aligned with the interests of headquarters. Decentralization in the area of decision making is obligatory in multinationals and has many advantages. However, it also means taking the risk that the subsidiaries' decisions may not be in line with corporate interests. To manage and reduce this risk, you (as headquarters) need to introduce control mechanisms that promote "correct" attitudes and behaviors (i.e. in line with your goals and interests) in the subsidiary. There are three basic mechanisms: monitoring, incentives, and socialization.

Make the subsidiary's control systems adequate. In the first steps of the life of a subsidiary, much flexibility and initiative are required to adapt the company's products and policies to the local environment. At this stage, introducing many operating and administrative controls can impede the subsidiary managers' ability to do their work efficiently. In these circumstances and also when many asymmetries of information exist (e.g. due to cultural distance, or to specialized knowledge in the subsidiary), it is better to rely on incentives and designate a certain proportion to be variable based on results.

Do not assume that incentives always work. Incentives function better the more measurable and controllable the outcomes are that the subsidiary is expected to fulfill. If there are many uncontrollable factors (e.g. volatility in the host country, economic recession), the managers and employees will assume a great deal of risk and we need to compensate them by offering a greater reward.

Do not rely solely on monetary incentives. Encouraging employees to identify with the organization and avoiding incongruence of objectives between the subsidiary and headquarters is a third form of control referred to as socialization. If you ensure that objectives are highly congruent, there will be less need for monitoring and incentives.

Promote a climate of cooperation among the company's units. Your challenge (as a manager of a multinational company) is to identify and disseminate best practices, regardless of where they originate. This is a noble objective, but one that is very difficult to implement unless we create a climate of cooperation among the various units of the multinational. Without this climate, it will be difficult for your firm to break down the barriers of distance, language, and culture that stand between employees of different units and to avoid having them focus on their own unit to the exclusion of the rest of the organization. This climate can be promoted by means of various compensation systems and corporate integration programs.

Examine what can motivate employees to accept an international assignment and to devote their maximum effort to it. Given the existence of multiple barriers to international mobility, a commonly used method of motivating employees is to offer them generous compensation packages. This policy can have a series of counterproductive effects and impede other objectives of the compensation system. There are other factors (e.g. acquiring international experience, improving career prospects) that can motivate international assignees as much as, or even more than, financial compensation.

Evaluate the impact that their policies for international assignments have on the attitudes and behavior of host country nationals. Of course, we want to attract, retain, and motivate international personnel, but we also want to do the same with local personnel, and the two goals are not independent of each other. The generous incentives designed to help attract employees to international service often have the effect of creating large pay gaps between expatriates and local employees. The less fortunate position of the local employee relative to that of the expatriate can impede the motivation of local employees and reduce their commitment to the organization. As we have seen, there are several initiatives that can contribute to preventing this from occurring.

Notes

1 KFC (Japan) Limited. Harvard Business School; n. 9-387-043, Rev: December 30, 1992.

2 KFC (Japan) Limited, n. 1 above.

3 Trepo, G. (1973) Management Style à La Francaise. *European Business*, Autumn, 71–79.

4 Schneider, S. (1986). National vs. Corporate Culture: Implications for HRM. *Human Resource Management* 27(1): 133–148.

5 Welsh, D., Luthans, F. and Sommer, S. (1993). Managing Russian Factory Workers: The Impact of U.S. Based Behavioral and Participative Techniques. *Academy of Management Journal* 36: 58–79.

6 Kovack, R. (1994). Matching Assumptions to Environment in the Transfer of Management Practices.

Performance Appraisal in Hungary. *International Studies of Management and Organisation* 24(4): 83–99.

7 Laurent, A. (1983). The Cultural Diversity of Western Management Conceptions. *International Studies of Management and Organisation* 8(1–2): 75–96.

8 The Nokia corporate website. http://www.nokia.com/corporate-responsibility/cr-report-2007/employees/embedding-our-values.

9 Guzzo, R. A., Noonan, K. A., and Elron, E. (1993). Employer influence on the expatriate experience: Limits and implications for retention in overseas assignments. *Research in Personnel and Human Resources Management* Suppl 3, 323–338.

10 KFC (Japan) Limited, n. 1 above.

11 This theory was developed long ago by Adolph Berle and Gardner Means (*The Modern Corporation and Private Property* (New York: MacMillan, 1932)) to explain the problems of corporate governance that stem from the inconsistency between ownership and control in public organizations. This theoretical framework has been extended to all those situations in which decision-making authority is delegated, such as those that occur in relations between employer and employee, lawyer and client and, also, between the headquarters of a multinational and each of its subsidiaries. For instance, see Watson O'Donnell, S. (2000). Managing Foreign Subsidiaries: Agents of HQs, or an independent network? *Strategic Management Journal* 21: 525–548.

12 Bonache, J. (2000). The international transfer of an idea suggestion system: against radical relativism in international human resource management. *International Studies of Management and Organization* 29(4): 24–44.

13 Philips versus Matsushita: A New Century, a New Round. Harvard Business School; no. 9-302-049, January 17, 2008.

14 P&G Japan: The SK-II Globalization Project, Harvard Buiness School; no, 9-303-003.

15 Philips versus Matsushita, A New Century, n. 13 above.

16 By this term economists refer to a type of behavior, such as lying, stealing, cheating, and making calculated efforts to mislead, distort, disagree, obfuscate, or otherwise confuse. This behavior occurs when people are driven by self-interest, no matter how detrimental their attitude can be to others, and whenever such a behavior is not easy to detect by a third party.

17 Bonache, J. and Cerviño, J. (1997). Global Integration without expatriates. *Human Resource Management Journal* 7(3): 89–100.

18 Philips versus Matsushita, A New Century, n. 13 above.

19 The Swiffer dry mop, a waterless car-washing cloth, or a washing machine-based dry cleaning product are some examples of those products (see P&G Japan, n. 14 above).

20 See, for instance, Gomez Mejia, L., Balkin, D., and Cardy, R., *Managing Human Resources* (Chapter 12, "Rewarding Performance") (New York: Prentice Hall, 1995).

21 Cyert, R. and March, J., *A Behavioral Theory of the Firm* (Englewood Cliffs, NJ: Prentice Hall, 1963).

22 Silvio Napoli at Schindler India, HBS No. 302-054.

23 Ouchi, W.G. (1979): A conceptual Framework for the design of organizational control mechanisms. *Management Science* 25: 833–848.

24 Silvio Napoli at Schindler India, n. 22 above.

25 Bonache, J. (2008). La función de recursos humanos en la internacionalización del Santander: Objetivos, logros y retos. *Universia Business Review* 15: 76–89.

26 See, for example, Selmer, J. (2004). Expatriates' hesitation and the localization of Western business operations in China. *International Journal of Human Resource Management* 15(6) 1094–1197.

27 Fey, C. and Fury, P. (2008). Top Management Incentive Compensation and knowledge sharing in Multinational Corporations. *Strategic Management Journal* 29: 1301–1323.

28 2002 Worldwide Survey of International Assignment Policies and Practices, European Edition, Organization Resources Counselors.

29 Yet there also exist solutions to this problem. For example, Endesa, a Spanish electrical company, gets around this problem by giving all peer-group expatriates the same host country element, such as housing or goods and services allowances.

30 Reynolds, C. (1997). Expatriate Compensation in Historical Perspective. *Journal of World Business* 32(2): 118–132.

31 Chen, C. C., Choi, J., and Chi, S. C. (2002). Making justice sense of local-expatriate compensation disparity: Mitigation by local referents, ideological explanations, and interpersonal sensitivity in China-foreign joint ventures. *Academy of Management Journal* 45(4): 807–826.

32 Global Relocation Trends: 2003/2004 Survey Report. Electronic version: www.gmacglobalrelocation.com/2003survey.

33 Along these lines, some recent studies (e.g. Gong, 2003) have shown a positive effect of expatriate staffing on the performance of culturally distant units, especially at their early stages.

34 Bonache, J. and Pla, J. (1995). When are international managers a cost effective solution? The rationale of transaction costs economics applied to staffing decisions in MNCs. *Journal of Business Research* 26: 112–131.

35 Jaques, E., *Equitable Payment* (New York: John Wiley and Sons Inc., 1961) and Stacy Adams, J. (1963) Toward an Understanding of Inequity. *Journal of Abnormal and Social Psychology* 67: 422–436.

36 The analysis we present is based on the following works: Toh, S. M. and DeNisi, A. (2003). Host country national reactions to expatriates pay policies: A model and implications. *Academy of Management Review* 28(4): 606–621; Chen, C. C., Choi, J., and Chi, S. C., n. 31 above; Bonache, J., Sanchez, J., and Zarraga, C. (2009). The Interaction of Expatriate Pay Differential and Expatriate Inputs on Host Country Nationals' Pay Unfairness. *The International Journal of HRM*, vol. 20, October, 2132–2146.

37 Shapiro, D. L. and Brett, J. M. (1993). Comparing three processes underlying judgements of procedural justice: A field study of mediation and arbitration. *Journal of Personality and Social Psychology* 65(6): 1167–1177.

38 Guzzo, R.A., Noonan, K.A., and Elron, E., n. 9 above.

39 Hackman, J. and Oldham, G. (1976). Motivation through the design of work: Test of a theory. *Organizational Behavior and Human Performance* 16: 250–279.

40 For an excellent review of factors contributing to expatriates' career success, see Bolino, M. C. (2007). Expatriate assignments and intraorganizational career success: implications for individuals and organizations. *Journal of International Business Studies* 38(5): 819–835.

41 Daily, C. M., Certo, S. T., and Dalton, D. R. (2000). International experience in the executive suite: The path to prosperity? *Strategic Management Journal* 21(4): 515–523.

42 Borman, W. C. and Motowidlo, S. J. (1993). "Expanding the criteria domain to include elements of contextual performance" in N. Schmitt and W. C. Borman & Associates (eds), *Personnel selection in organizations* (San Francisco: Jossey-Bass, 1993), pp. 71–98.

CHAPTER 8
Conclusions

8.1 Framing the Challenges, Issues and Decisions for Managing the Global Workforce

This book was written to offer a framework for understanding the complexities of managing the global workforce. The book was not intended to be fully comprehensive – as it would be almost impossible (and already outdated at the time of publication) to offer every possible legal, economic, and sociopolitical factor one may encounter in each country and for every strategic goal desired by companies from diverse industries, with diverse competitive reasons for having a global workforce in the first place. Instead, the book was intended to offer a framework for understanding the challenges and issues one must address and the decisions one must make when managing human talent worldwide.

8.2 The Foundational Global Issues for Managing the Global Workforce

The framework is based on three foundational issues: global business strategy, comparative HR systems, and cross-cultural issues. It was a conscious decision to begin with the company's global business strategy in Chapter 2, as it provides managers with a guide for the way to approach all subsequent global workforce decisions. Global firms are highly complex, with continued concurrent strategic pressures to be both integrated globally and responsive locally. No two companies will have identical approaches to the strategic decisions along this global versus local continuum. And, for this reason, companies will need to manage their global workforce in ways that best fit their strategic needs and the contextual demands of the countries where they operate.

As illustrated in many of the cases included in this book, managers need to consider the global versus local strategic needs of the firm, but they must also consider the contextual issues as well as each country's HR systems and culture, and how these factors affect their strategic needs. It is important to remember that a company's global business strategy, while the important first step, needs to be understood within the contextual bounds of each foreign subsidiary's offshoring provider, or plant location's HR system and culture.

Our framework in this book was built with the two contextual foundational issues, comparative HR systems in Chapter 3 and cultural issues in Chapter 4. While business strategy is set forth by the organization to guide global workforce decisions, the HR system is a fixed aspect of the contextual environment. In every country there will be a distinct set of workforce competencies, labor economics, employment laws, and employee representation. These represent the contextual backdrop for managing the global workforce as they are the diverse country-level environments in which talent is managed.

Chapter 4 focused on cross-cultural differences, describing the cultural dimensions that influence the acceptance of global human resource practices, such as cross-cultural differences in management styles, time, communication, and the like. This chapter encouraged you to move beyond a mere academic understanding of cultural differences and understand when to leverage them and when to override them from the perspective of business strategy. We encourage all managers to be very clear on the cross-national differences in the ways individuals gain trust and credibility, communicate, and work together. These collectively will influence your ability to be effective in the countries where you work.

8.3   The Human Resource Decisions for Managing the Global Workforce

The second half of Global Dimensions of Human Resource Management applies the three foundational areas concurrently when considering the key practice areas of HRM. Winning in the global arena will largely depend on how well firms can leverage, attract, develop, engage, and motivate the strategic capabilities of their human talent globally. As Figure 1.1 illustrated in Chapter 1, there is a balance that must be struck in the way talent is managed globally to accomplish the work necessary for the effective functioning of the organization – in the context of the HR systems and cultures in the countries where the firm operates.

The first way to manage talent is to design work to leverage the global reach and strategic needs of the firm. We described in Chapter 5 how global organizations manage the global mobility of their people (e.g. expatriates), the global mobility of jobs (e.g. offshoring), and the global mobility of knowledge (e.g. transnational teams). These three moving pieces – people, jobs, and knowledge – combine to form the structure in which human resource management practices are delivered globally.

The effective management of the competencies, attitudes, and behaviors of the global talent are the final pieces of the framework. Chapter 6 described challenges in managing the competencies of the global workforce (i.e. recruitment, selection, training, and development) and Chapter 7 highlighted the challenges in managing their attitudes and behaviors (e.g. compensation and motivation). In both chapters we highlight a few of the cross-national and comparative issues to help raise awareness of the breadth of challenges when making human talent decisions in various countries around the world.

Following the discussion of the various decisions, each of these chapters included a segment on managing international assignees. We opted to include a larger segment on international assignees in both chapters because, as a group, their competencies, attitudes, and behaviors can greatly influence a firm's competitiveness globally. They are, as they should be, generally managed in a way which reflects the high level of influence they can have globally.

8.4 The Human Resource Management Function Globally

With a focus on the management of global talent, it is important to consider the various strategic imperatives from which firms operate and the corresponding strategies influencing human resources. We have discussed the various national and cultural influences which may affect how HR is managed. In particular, we consider the way in which firms structure their human resource functions and specific human resource management practices around the world. A key issue for managing the global workforce is to determine which HR practices should be controlled from headquarters and which should be local. Mirroring the strategy of firms, there are some elements of the HR function which tend to be controlled through headquarters and some which tend to be more locally controlled. Once the overall desired structure of HR worldwide is determined on the basis of global business strategy, specific HR practices follow – based on country-level HR systems, cross-cultural differences, and work design (for the flow of people, jobs, and knowledge).

There are some HR activities that tend to be centrally controlled across firms, regardless of strategic perspective or need for given strategic capabilities. Two factors influencing whether HR practices will be centrally controlled are (1) a firm's desire to manage key assets and (2) a firm's need to minimize cost. For example, the worldwide selection and succession planning for the firm's top management team or critical employees (e.g. research scientists in R&D firms) will often be centrally controlled because these key individuals are considered the firm's critical resources. Stock allocation is also controlled centrally because the firm's stock is also a finite corporate resource. Many mature global firms purport to have a unified ethical code of conduct and, as such, the training and communications associated with maintaining ethical standards tend to be generated from headquarters. Other large-scale HR initiatives, such as global HR Information Systems, are increasingly more centrally controlled in an effort to leverage the economies of scale across the subsidiaries around the world.

There are many HR activities that have been traditionally carried out locally. The predominant reason for the localization of certain HR practices, as we discussed in Chapter 3, is the connection to a given country's HR system. Thus, HR activities such as employee and labor relations and the disbursement of medical and health benefits tend to be locally driven. Other HR activities that require face time, such as an ombudsperson, are also more commonly conducted locally. Highly administrative tasks, such as the staffing production positions and payroll administration also tend to be conducted locally.

Many activities within the human resource function do not readily fall into a category of either local control or headquarters control – rather they represent true global resources which may be organized and applied differentially depending on the situation of the firm. To capitalize on economies of scale, these activities are ever-expanding in most human resource functions across firms today. They include centers of excellence, shared services, HR service centers, and outsourced HR activities.

The contextual differences described in this book will have an influence on the way in which human resource policies and practices are developed and implemented. In some cases, human resource practices are an outgrowth of a country's cultural values. For example, diversity management and stock options reflect the American cultural dimensions of receptivity to differences and individual orientation, respectively. Quality circles and open office space reflect the Japanese cultural dimensions of group orientation. Cultural challenges can be partially anticipated in multinational firms where human resource practices may be developed in one country and transferred to others.

HR practices may be shaped by cultural differences. When common global HR practices are needed, many multinational firms assign HR teams with cross-national representation to collectively develop practices that will be implemented on a worldwide basis. Alternatively, some firms are allowing for local variation in HR practices developed at headquarters. The practice of local adaptation is generally effective provided the spirit of a given practice is maintained. Another approach altogether is to allow the HR function to be an entirely local function. Admittedly, this is a more difficult approach when firm-level assets are being considered. For example, leaders' succession planning is often conducted with some global coordination because leaders are generally part of a global talent pool – a shared firm asset.

Global Mobility and Global Talent Management. While often located down the same corridor in the Human Resources wing of most corporate headquarters, the directors of global or international mobility and talent management lead their respective complementary, but not often strategically integrated, functions. As complementary HR functions, talent development professionals identify the firm's talent deemed to be ready for international assignments, when (and sometimes where) they should be assigned, and what they will be expected to do. Once talent has been identified, global mobility professionals manage the myriad of complexities (and vendors) – everything from their tax and visas to the movement of their household goods and international schools. In these complementary roles, the collaboration is generally minimal once a prospective international assignee is handed off from the talent management professionals to the global mobility professionals. As a matter of practicality, there is some efficiency-based value in global mobility and talent management operating as complementary HR functions (especially in firms with international assignee populations predominantly placed in less developmental – and more technical and functional – assignments).

While efficient, global mobility and talent management operating in complementary HR functions is, however, *rarely effective* from the perspective of global HR strategy. In brief, there is a growing strategic need in most firms to produce more culturally agile leaders through systematic global leadership development programs. This strategic HR need has led to a paradigm shift, as the global mobility and talent management functions are being reconfigured to be more strategically integrated HR partners.

As strategically integrated HR partners, both talent management and global mobility professionals work together under one set of strategic business goals guiding where international assignees should be placed and why. For example, as strategically integrated HR partners, the talent management professionals have a deeper knowledge of the specific global competencies needing to be developed for any given high potential; they are able to readily identify who is predisposed to achieve the desired developmental gains from a given international assignment. Global mobility professionals, also operating as strategically integrated HR partners, possess the same knowledge of the desired developmental global competencies, and, in turn, are able to design international assignments with associated support practices to increase the probability of the desired developmental competencies being gained.

In firms where the global mobility and talent management functions operate as strategically integrated HR partners, three elements are recognized by both functions: (1) not all international assignments are intentionally developmental, (2) not all individuals have the ability to develop from the experience of international assignments, and (3) the completion of an assignment is not the same as gaining desired developmental competencies. These three elements represent a significant paradigm shift within the HR function. This change seems to be affecting talent management and global mobility professionals equally, as they both need to gain new knowledge about the repertoire of possible developmental competencies potentially inherent in international assignments, how to craft the experiences to elicit those developmental competencies, and how to identify talent most likely to experience the developmental gain. Given the speed of globalization and the need for culturally agile associates, the time is right for the integration of talent management and international mobility.

Conclusions

Corporations' competitiveness on a global scale is largely contingent on firms' abilities to strategically adapt, reconfigure, and acquire the resources needed for the ever-changing global marketplace. Given that it is the people within organizations who sell and market, develop products, make decisions, and implement programs, human resources are vital to the success of an organization. We hope that the material and cases in this book served to highlight how the management of human talent worldwide and that the application of human resource practices congruent with the organizations' strategic plans can help manifest the firms' strategic capabilities, and be a means to facilitate the successful implementation of firms' global business strategies.

INDEX